A VIEW TO THE FUTURE

Dedicated to all those staff, past and present,
who contributed so much to the JT business and ethos.

A VIEW TO THE FUTURE

JT Group
a radical approach to building and development

Roland Adburgham

 redcliffe

First published in 2006 by Redcliffe Press Ltd., 81g Pembroke Road, Bristol BS8 3EA
www.www.redcliffepress.co.uk

© 2006 Roland Adburgham
Original photography © Stephen Morris

ISBN 1 904537 42 1

British Library Cataloguing-in-Publication Data
A catalogue record for this book is available from the British Library

Designed and typeset by Stephen Morris smc@freeuk.com
Printed by HSW Tonypandy

Contents

Photo-credits: the publishers apologize to, and would be pleased to hear from, any copyright holders who feel they have not been adequately acknowledged.

JT – urban transformation in practice

In 1961 John Pontin and Tim Organ got together in Bristol to start their own design/build company and the rest is history. JT transformed itself from a tiny operation into a company of over £50 million turnover in the space of 28 years. This book traces its growth and consolidation in the historical context in which it occurred, and describes the company's philosophy. Above all else it seeks to describe why JT became an extraordinary success story that continues, though in a new form, till today.

John Pontin explains the unique formula that underpinned JT's success with clients: 'We have recognised that providing clients with the right building, on time and within budget, can be most readily achieved when architect, engineer, quantity surveyor, project manager and other essential skills work together as a team, removing traditional professional barriers.'

From the outset, a form of lateral thinking was a key feature of the company's approach – even before the term was coined. JT soon made a name for itself both for the quality of its work and its generosity of spirit. An important part of the company's philosophy was to encourage staff to think for themselves and for the entire enterprise, and to share in its success.

'To attract and retain good people, a company must create the right environment in all respects. From the outset, JT had its own special culture, based on informality, flexibility and positive encouragement to take responsibility. This has created a climate where corporate loyalty is strong, and hard work is both a way of life and enjoyable.'

John Pontin emerges as the driving force behind a highly innovative enterprise – innovative not only in combining design and building in one multi-layered company but also in social purpose. John knows about using the power of strategic investments to bring about social change. Before long JT started supporting socially and culturally beneficial activities. It is very unusual for an entrepreneur who creates a brand new company also to become a force for positive change in society within a few years.

The story of Bush House in Prince Street, the imposing building that came to house both the Arnolfini Gallery and JT's offices, is another example of 'transformation in practice.' Like in so many other cities after the war, Bristol had lost the use of its river port and with it the throbbing heart of the city.

Transforming a run-down yet palatial building in a riverside location and developing it in partnership with an art gallery was to turn a problem site into a major asset for Bristol. The Arnolfini's reopening after extensive refurbishment in September 2005 was a significant moment for Bristol and the South-West.

Across the river from Bush House, JT brought about further transformations. Converting disused harbourside buildings in Canon's Road to new uses was another example of enlightened property development. The Watershed arts venue and the new pubs, restaurants and shops along the riverfront have become a key feature of central Bristol's urban fabric. JT was also centrally involved in the building of Pero's bridge, a cantilevered structure that connects the two sides of the old harbour.

John Pontin has developed a unique way of building harmonious bridges between business and charitable activities of social value. His chairmanship of the Dartington Hall Trust was a significant part of this personal journey. Again and again John succeeded in combining business acumen with significant social and cultural benefit. This spirit is what much of this book is about. It was fascinating for me to find out about aspects of JT's work that I had not been aware of. Having known John for some 20 years as a highly creative person, I now know much more about how he connects doing well with doing good and why he was awarded his OBE. Seeing the big picture of a world that needs transformation, he has found very specific ways of creating effective change.

John, with his endlessly curious mind, always seeks new horizons. His support of the Natural Step, started in Sweden by Dr. Karl-Henrik Robert, has been instrumental in getting this important initiative to become internationally effective. John's support for the Schumacher Society, which holds the annual Bristol Schumacher Lectures – Britain's 'premier environmental gathering', according to *The Guardian* – has been invaluable. The new 'Schumacher Institute for Sustainable Systems' also benefits from John's support.

John Pontin's growing concern for the sustainable and socially beneficial development of Bristol and the world beyond keeps taking on new guises. His latest idea is the urban redevelopment company Under the Sky. His key idea is that there are sites and buildings in Bristol and the West of England that need to be transformed for the benefit of the community but are outside the normal scope of private developers, housing associations or other organisations. Under the Sky, then, is intended to be another agent in urban transformation – turning underused yet potentially valuable sites into community assets.

This book is an intriguing story of transformation – of a young man into a successful entrepreneur, of a young company into a major player in building design and construction, and of the application of a creative mind to the problems of urban regeneration. It may help the reader in his or her own transformation into a person truly useful and beneficial to society.

Herbert Girardet
Chairman, Schumacher Society
Director, Under the Sky
Director of Research, World Future Council Initiative

1 The way we built
Style and practice through time

The history of architecture is the history of the world. The belief and manners of all people are embodied in the edifices they raised. Augustus Pugin (1812-52)

No person expects his or her life to exceed 100 years but what is built by humans has at least the potential to last for centuries. 'When we build, let us think we build for ever,' wrote John Ruskin, in *The Seven Lamps of Architecture* (1849). That could always be wishful, rather than achievable, but what has been built is the mark of our civilisation. A century ago, John Belcher, when president of the Royal Institute of British Architects (RIBA), stated: 'Architecture recounts the past, records the present, and holds up ideals for the future.' Then and now, history is relevant to revive and renew our towns and cities.

The earliest surviving structures date back several thousand years and even today cause wonder at the skills of their builders. Remnants of the early civilisations during the Stone, Bronze and Iron Ages can still be seen around many parts of the British Isles. The Romans, who occupied the country from AD43 until 410, left much evidence of their construction skills with the invention of cement to make concrete and the use of stone, brick, tiles and mosaics. Concrete – to be the most widely used material in the world for present-day buildings – made it possible for Roman architecture to be more inventive.

After the retreat of the Romans, a turbulent way of life lasted for several centuries during the misnamed Dark Ages. Rural habitation was preferred rather than the town planning of the Romans and concrete was forgotten. Timber structures built then would be lost in time but there was accomplished craftsmanship: exquisite artefacts were found in the burial site at Sutton Hoo in Suffolk. 'Despite the initial brutality of the pagan Angles and Saxons who invaded Britain in the fifth and sixth centuries…an Anglo-Saxon culture was established by 700 which made Britain the most civilised country in Europe,' wrote David Watkin (*A History of Western Architecture*, Barrie & Jenkins 1986). 'Though Anglo-Saxon secular architecture was largely of timber, Roman missionaries introduced a new type of brick and stone building from the Mediterranean and Gaul.'

Churches and buildings, however, were to suffer destruction by the marauding Vikings from Scandinavia. That era ended in 1066 when the Anglo-Saxons were subjugated by the Normans – who themselves were of a mixed Scandinavian and Frankish race. Castles to dominate the Anglo-Saxons were built of moats, timber defences and earth ramparts and then with stone. In 1086, the Domesday Book was a survey and valuation of landed property and the feudal system lasted for several centuries.

Master builders

In the Norman times, master builders and master masons came from France to create abbeys, monasteries and Romanesque cathedrals. From about 1200 to 1500, during the Gothic periods – described as Early English, Decorated and Perpendicular – masons learned skills to build churches with rib-vaulted ceilings, buttresses and pointed arches. Sculptures, gargoyles and stained-glass windows decorated churches and manor houses became less fortified. Francis Bacon (1561-1626), in his essay *Of Building*, said: 'Houses are built to live in, and not to look on; therefore let use be preferred before uniformity, except where both may be had. Leave the goodly fabrics of houses, for beauty only...You shall have sometimes fair houses so full of glass, that one cannot tell where to become, to be out of the sun or cold.'

The Renaissance revived the largely forgotten architectural heritage of Rome and Greece and changed the visual character of cities. 'The classic order once more established an intellectual ascendancy, not seriously challenged until the latter half of the 19th century,' wrote Arthur Stratton (*The Orders of Architecture*, Studio Editions 1986.) Designs were influenced by the technical treatise *De Architectura*, written by the Roman architect Vitruvius, with the five orders of classical columns:

> Doric, the earliest order with plain or fluted shaft and plain capital.
>
> Ionic, plain or fluted shaft with a scroll-like capital.
>
> Corinthian, plain or fluted shaft, sculptured foliage in the capital.
>
> Tuscan, an unfluted shaft, similar to Doric.
>
> Composite, a variant of Ionic and Corinthian.

John Gloag, the social historian of architecture and design, wrote: 'The architect, fundamentally an artist and secondarily an organiser, was recognised as the master designer; the controller and collator of all work connected with building, from the initial planning down to the smallest ornamental details within and without.' (*The Architectural Interpretation of History*, A. & C. Black 1975) An architect could be equally a master builder – the 'master builder' defined from 1557 by the *Oxford English Dictionary* as 'one who is skilled in the art of building, an architect.' Architect, defined from 1563, was 'a master builder, specifically one whose profession is to prepare plans of edifices, and exercise a general superintendence over their erection.' Collaborative planning, design, management and construction could be interpreted as 'design and build', a term not then adopted. The shared practice would be lost in the Victorian period and not revived until the 1960s, when the JT company was started.

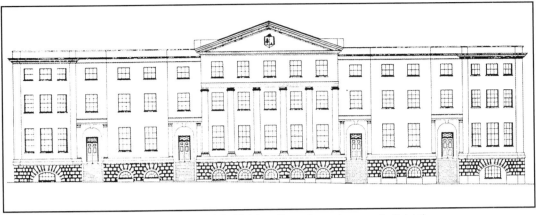

Clifton Hotel and Assembly Rooms, The Mall. Eighteenth-century elegance in Bristol.

Until the Victorian times, architects depended upon patronage and were associated with artists to complete their creations. 'No person who is not a great sculptor or painter can be an architect,' said Ruskin. 'If he is not a sculptor or a painter, he can only be a builder.' Inigo Jones (1573-1652), adopting the style of Andrea Palladio, designed the Banqueting House in Whitehall. The ceiling was painted by Rubens commissioned by Charles I, who was executed there after the civil war. Much of London was to be devastated by the 1666 fire, witnessed by Samuel Pepys: 'The churches, houses, and all on fire and flaming at once; and a horrid noise the flames made, and the cracking of houses at their ruin.' It was realised that the city must be reconstructed with brick and stone houses, not wooden, and that there should be effective fire protection and buildings insurance. Christopher Wren, in a Baroque style, rebuilt many of the destroyed churches and St Paul's Cathedral, while the younger Nicholas Hawksmoor and John Vanbrugh designed Baroque churches and country houses.

The Georgian period began from 1720 with architects achieving handsome buildings:

Robert Adam: houses and interiors; shop-lined Pulteney Bridge in Bath inspired by fourteenth century Ponte Vecchio in Florence.

John Wood and his son John: Bath's Royal Crescent, Queen Square and Circus.

John Soane: Bank of England and Dulwich Picture Gallery.

William Chambers: Somerset House, now the home of Courtauld Institute of Art's collections.

John Nash: Brighton Pavilion with oriental domes and minarets; white stucco terraces which adorn Regent's Park.

Country houses for landed gentry were created by architects when roads were improved for stage and mail coaches, making it possible for the rich to travel from their townhouses in private carriages. Most town properties, though, were mainly speculative by master builders, assisted by draughtsmen and surveyors, invoking 'pattern-book' designs. These resulted in the squares and terraces, with uniform dignity and fine period detail, that are deservedly appreciated today.

Industrial Revolution

The Royal Society of Arts (RSA) was formed in 1754 as The Royal Society for the Encouragement of Arts, Manufactures and Commerce, set up to 'embolden enterprise, to enlarge science, to refine art, to improve manufacture and to extend our commerce.' It reported that as early as 1770 it had looked for solutions to reduce smoke emissions and to plant trees because of severe deforestation. Today, its manifesto includes 'moving towards a zero waste society', with the RSA supporting the West of England's zero waste project initiated by John Pontin, JT Group's chairman and a fellow of the society.

In 1776, Adam Smith's *The Wealth of Nations* laid the intellectual foundations for free trade and economic expansion. The Industrial Revolution gathered pace with engineering and steam-powered machinery; steam engines pumped water and drained mines and, with the introduction of winding engines, more collieries were opened. Coking coal produced iron and steel and the output rapidly rose in the coalfields, as well as in the tin and copper mines of Cornwall and west Devon. An elaborate network of canals enabled barges to transport raw materials and heavy goods. Ironbridge in Shropshire, built in 1779 by Abraham Darby, became the first use of cast-iron in industrial architecture.

Royal and aristocratic power declined as the industrial, commercial and urban age evolved. The United Kingdom of Great Britain and Ireland was unified in 1801 (the year the London Stock Exchange was founded.) The population in England and Wales was counted to be only nine million and seven out of 10 people still lived in the countryside. But the population increased rapidly and the enclosure of communal agricultural land spurred the migration of cheap labour to newly industrialised cities. Pioneers in civil engineering were John McAdam, John Rennie and Thomas Telford, who became the first president of the Institution of Civil Engineers formed in 1818. Steam locomotives led to George Stephenson's Rocket in 1829 and the birth of the railways.

Only a few entrepreneurs were philanthropists willing to minimise the exploitation of labour. The first to be acknowledged was Robert Owen, who in managing the cotton mill at New Lanark, near Glasgow, transformed life for the local community. (It is now a world heritage site) He wrote *A New View of Society* to call for social change which helped to spawn the Factory Act of 1819, seeking to limit children's work in the mills. No factory inspectors, though, were appointed until 1833 and working conditions continued to be close to slavery. It was not until that year that an Act of Parliament abolished Britain's slave trade, which had flourished in the ports of London, Liverpool and Bristol.

Soon after Queen Victoria came to the throne in 1837, Flora Tristan, the French socialist writer and grandmother of Paul Gauguin, came to England and was shocked by the dreadful conditions of the working classes in comparison with France. She wrote: 'There is no law to prevent factory-owners from disposing of the youth and strength of their workers exactly as they please, purchasing their existence, sacrificing their very lives, just for the sake of making money.' (*The London Journal of Flora Tristan*, Virago 1982). This was no exaggeration. In 1845, the *Bradford Observer* reported: 'There are scores of wretched hovels, unfurnished and unventilated, damp, filthy in the extreme…No sewers, no drainage, no ventilation. Nothing to be seen but squalid wretchedness on every side.'

Bradford's population had soared to 100,000 people, with some 200 factory chimneys churning out sulphurous smoke. Workers' back-to-back cottages in the grimy industrial towns were primitive while mansions were built for their wealthy factory and mill employers. Benjamin Disraeli, in his novel *Sybil* (1845), wrote of the 'dank and dismal dwellings' of milltown life and that 'the privileged and the people formed two nations.' Charles Dickens' novel *Hard Times* (1854) was set in the fictional but credible Coketown – 'It was a town of red brick, or of brick that would have been red if the smoke and ashes had allowed it; but as matters stood it was a town of unnatural red and black like the painted face of a savage.'

Titus Salt, who owned textile mills in Bradford, followed the example of the Halifax mill owner Edward Akroyd, who improved the living standards of his workers by starting a model industrial village in 1850. Salt built a mill with a technology to lessen pollution and a community called Saltaire for his workers' homes with gas lighting, heating and fresh water. (Today, the restored mill has an art gallery with works by the Bradford-born David Hockney) Towns and cities, though, suffered from coal-burning pollution, aggravated by the mists and fogs of the climate. London was especially affected. By the mid-century, its seething population had reached four million, making it the world's largest city. The capital's lack of domestic plumbing and sewers caused three epidemics of cholera with 31,000 deaths being recorded. In response, the Metropolitan Board of Works was established in 1856 to supervise public works and its chief engineer, Joseph Bazalgette, organised an 82-mile underground network of sewers. In 1863, the first London underground railway opened and, as the network grew, the building of suburbs proliferated.

Architects as professionals

By the mid-nineteenth century, Britain was a world power with its industrial, trading and colonial empire. 'It was the balance between political stability and economic drive which was the secret of Victorian Britain – for without the first the second could be rapidly undermined,' wrote Anthony Sampson (*The Changing Anatomy of Britain*, Hodder &

Saltaire: Titus Salt's vision of working-class comfort.

Stoughton 1982). The professions were formed to meet national ambitions. The roles of architect, engineer, surveyor and master builders were separately defined as construction intensified and contracts became more legalistic.

RIBA was founded in 1834, the same year as the Chartered Institute of Building, which describes itself today as 'the leading professional body worldwide for managers in construction.' The Architectural Association, the oldest independent school of architecture in the UK, was founded in 1847 as an 'endeavour towards an improved system of architectural study' at a time when there was no formal training. The journal *The Builder* was published from 1842 (renamed *Building*) and the General Builders Association began in 1865, to be succeeded by the National Association of Master Builders. The Institution of Surveyors, formed in 1868, evolved into the Royal Institution of Chartered Surveyors.

Some of today's construction companies have their origins during those times. Mowlem was founded as early as 1822 by John Mowlem and Laing began when James Laing and his wife built themselves a home in Cumbria in 1848. The widening distinction between architect and builder was partly a matter of social class: architects were likely to have been educated at independent public schools while most builders had left school at 14 or younger. Isambard Kingdom Brunel – educated in Paris – was an engineer with scientific knowledge and a range of talents which could not be emulated as design and

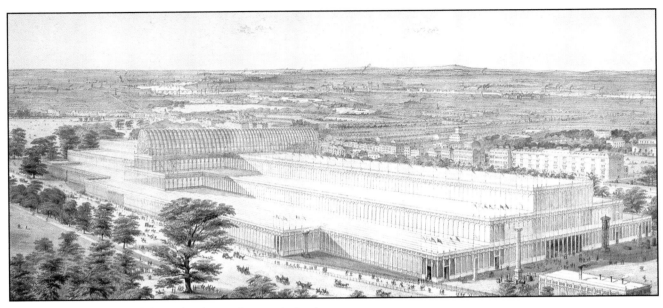

Joseph Paxton's Crystal Palace: drawing on the new technology.

technology grew more complex. Obsessively overworked, he died in 1859 when only 53. His work at Bristol – which over a century later was to be JT Group's home city – were visionary achievements: the original railway station at Temple Meads; Clifton suspension bridge over Avon Gorge; and ss *Great Britain*, his iron steamship which, launched in 1843, was the first to be powered by a screw propeller. (The ship, salvaged from where it had been abandoned in the Falkland Islands, returned in 1970 to its dry dock in Bristol's Floating Harbour).

Victorian grandeur

While the Victorian cities became ever more crowded, architects were little interested in town planning and chose to design individual, upper-class houses and public buildings. Councillors and capitalists wanted civic halls, monuments and parks to impress the citizens. Power and wealth were marked by elaborate town halls with imposing facades and decorative rooflines, as well as public libraries, museums, banks and statues of local worthies.

The list of leading proponents of Gothic Revival, endorsed by Ruskin, is impressive:

Charles Barry and Augustus Pugin – the Houses of Parliament.

George Gilbert Scott – Glasgow University, St Pancras Station and the Albert Memorial

William Wilkins – National Gallery

Robert Smirke – British Museum

Charles Cockerell – Ashmolean Museum.

Bishopston,
Bristol:
Victorian comfort.

Middle-class homebuyers favoured the ornate styles copied by their builders' pattern books and sought to move outwards to less densely populated places. 'Most of the Victorian cities expanded with restless disorder: they thrust out jagged points deep into rural areas, their direction often determined by that of a railway line,' wrote John Gloag in his book *Victorian Comfort* (A. & C. Black 1961). Those who appreciated aesthetic values deplored the urban banality. 'Forget the spreading of the hideous town; think rather of the pack-horse on the down,' wrote William Morris, in poetic but anachronistic fashion, and who trained as an architect.

Non-anachronistic designs drew on the resources of industrial production. Decimus Burton designed the Palm House at Kew, built in 1844, and Joseph Paxton created the Crystal Palace for the 1851 Great Exhibition in Hyde Park. Paxton had been inspired by the Amazonian lily, the ribs and cross-ribs supporting its huge leaf. He used prefabricated components of iron and glass to create an immense and graceful structure, covering 19 acres. Among the six million visitors was Charlotte Brontë who wrote: 'It is a wonderful place – vast, strange, new, and impossible to describe. Its grandeur does not consist in one thing, but in the unique assemblage of all things.' (Although intended as a temporary structure, the palace was dismantled and moved to South London. It was destroyed by fire in 1936.) Paxton's technique of iron pillars and cantilever girders was replicated in railway termini. Ironwork was also used to erect seaside piers of which Eugenius Birch, an engineer, was the most prolific designer. His Brighton West Pier, built in the mid 1860s, had sadly deteriorated by the late twentieth century: an indictment of official indifference to such elegant structures. Cast-iron and wrought-iron were superseded after Henry Bessemer patented a process of cheap and rapid production of steel.

More construction and civil engineering companies were founded. Richard Costain started his business in 1865, Robert McAlpine in 1869 and George Wimpey in the next decade, when the National Federation of Builders was established. Bovis was set up in 1885 and the Henry Boot Group in the following year. The division between building firms and the architectural profession was clearcut. Qualified architects, belonging to RIBA, would not be employed by the builders. Architects were in independent private practices, working on fee-based commissions for their clients. Once the client and architect had reached an agreement on the design, building firms were invited to tender for the construction contract. *The Oxford English Dictionary*, in an edition as late as 1964, defined a builder to be 'the master artisan, who is instructed by the architect, and employs the manual labourers.'

Designs for towns

In the latter part of the nineteenth century, traditional materials would still be sourced for local vernacular buildings:

> Stone, handmade brick, flint and cob.
> Tiles, slate and thatch.
> Timber for floors and rafters, also weatherboarding.
> Lath and plaster for walls and ceilings.

Materials, however, were being transported cheaply by rail across the country, lessening the individual visual character of cities, towns and villages. Slate, for example, would be brought from Wales and Cornwall and used instead of local clay tiles or stone roof slates.

Bedford Park, London.

A forerunner of garden suburbs was Bedford Park in west London, with Norman Shaw designing houses in a Queen Anne Revival style with red brick and white joinery. It was advertised as 'The healthiest place in the world.' *Suburban Homes of London* (1881), a residential guide, quoted the prospectus: 'It is believed that this estate represents the first endeavour to secure, in the erection of houses at moderate rents, good construction, with attention to artistic effect, coupled with most complete sanitary arrangements, both in their drainage and perfect freedom from sewer gas.'

Bedford Park was built close to a railway station so that residents could commute to work. But few other imaginative projects were conceived to co-ordinate employment with social and domestic life. One paternalistic project was by William Hesketh Lever, a Quaker who built a factory in 1889 with a model village next to the River Mersey. Called Port Sunlight and designed by William Owen, its tree-lined streets were laid out in a boulevard

Port Sunlight, soap magnate W.H. Lever's garden suburb in Cheshire, begun 1887. This courtyard was designed by his company architect, J. Lomax-Simpson in 1913.
[*A Pictorial History of English Architecture*, John Betjeman 1972]

fashion. Another example was a garden village next to the Cadbury Brothers factory at Bournville, Birmingham. George Cadbury, also a Quaker, said it should 'ameliorate the condition of the working-class and labouring population…by the provision of improved dwellings, with gardens and open space to be enjoyed.'

Towards the new century, architects began to introduce styles detached from the classical orders. The birth of the Arts & Crafts Movement, inspired by Ruskin and put into effect by William Morris, reflected distaste for mass production while seeking to idealise design, craftsmanship and art. Standen, a family house in West Sussex, designed by Philip Webb and decorated throughout by Morris, was a showpiece of that movement. It was eventually owned by the National Trust, which itself was founded in 1895. The movement became linked with Art Nouveau, as was Charles Rennie Mackintosh's design of Glasgow

School of Art. Its construction began in 1896, the year when *Architectural Review* was first published. One of the magazine's four founding partners was Edmund Abram (the grandfather of this author). *Architectural Review* – which today calls itself 'the world's favourite architectural magazine' – wrote in an article marking its centenary: 'Abram seems to have been the driving force – he was already a pioneer photo-journalist and had a strong belief that British architects and builders were not being properly served by the existing professional and trade papers.'

Town and country

At the start of the Edwardian period, after the death of Queen Victoria in 1901, the nation's population reached 38 million with 23 cities each having more than 100,000 inhabitants. In an attempt to integrate architecture into a community-based framework, Ebenezer Howard wrote a book republished as *Garden Cities of Tomorrow* in 1902 (Faber reprint). Howard had been influenced by his stay in Chicago, which became known as the 'Garden City' after it laid out parks in 1869. He wrote: 'There are in reality not only, as is so constantly assumed, two alternatives – town life and country life – but a third alternative, in which all the advantages of the most energetic and active town life, with all the beauty and delight of the country, may be secured in perfect combination.'

His concept was borne out in 1903, when Letchworth began as a garden city of parks, tree-lined streets and low-density housing. The land was leased by the whole community.

Vernacular housing at Letchworth, the first garden city, 1903.

The architects were Raymond Unwin and his cousin Barry Parker, who had been asked by Joseph Rowntree to design a model village next to his factory at New Earswick, near York. In 1905 they were commissioned by Henrietta Barnett to plan a second garden suburb, at Hampstead in north London. The aim, Unwin stated, was to give 'working people the opportunity of taking a cottage with a garden within a 2d. fare of Central London.' The suburb's Central Square was designed by Edwin Lutyens, who proved to be the most influential of the early twentieth-century architects. Unusually among leading architects, he designed many houses rather than public buildings, working in the English Renaissance style. In a different style, following the Arts & Crafts Movement, was Charles Voysey, his designs loosely imitated in what became known as 'mock tudor' suburban houses, with leaded windows, herring-bone brickwork and gabled porches.

Unwin published *Town Planning in Practice* in 1909 (Princeton Architectural Press reprint) and pressure to improve residential standards resulted that year in the first Housing & Town Planning Act. This enabled local authorities to regulate the layout and density of suburban development. The Royal Town Planning Institute was founded in 1914, which 'exists to advance the science and art of town planning for the benefit of the public.' Welwyn Garden City was created soon after the First World War by Ebenezer Howard and designed by Louis de Soissons, who was later to design houses for staff at Dartington Hall in Devon. But most architects wanted little involvement in domestic design. The garden suburbs were to be followed by builders' crude copies and, as was suggested in Rudyard Kipling's *A Truthful Song* (1910):

> "How very little, since things were made,
>   Things have altered in the building trade."

2 New ways, bad ways
A divisive industry

The physician can bury his mistakes, but the architect can only advise his clients to plant vines. Frank Lloyd Wright (1867-1959)

After the First World War, with its immense loss of young lives, the British Empire began to crumble. National self-confidence, which had marked the Victorian and Edwardian eras with flamboyant public buildings, dissipated. Before the war, construction had begun of the imposing County Hall designed by Ralph Knott in Edwardian Baroque style for London County Council. The war delayed the work and the hall was not officially opened until 1922 and even then far from completed. Two of the few other 'landmark' buildings of the post-war period were Wembley football stadium, with its famous twin towers – since demolished – and Wills Memorial Tower at Bristol University. The 215ft (65.5m) stone tower, designed by George Oatley, was one of the last great Gothic buildings in England.

Technology and manufacture were evolving fast in the motor and aviation industries, as were the methods of construction – but not in the practice of 'design and build' in Britain. A brickworks in Bedfordshire, where there was abundant clay, was started in 1898 and, as London Brick Company, it became the world's largest on a 221-acre site. Reinforced concrete, patented by François Hennebique at the turn of the century, together with steel, enabled the construction of high-rise offices and flats. Electric lifts were first installed in 1889 by Otis in New York and the escalator was invented two years later by an American, Jesse W. Reno. In New York, steel-framed buildings were being built and the 21-storey Flatiron, constructed in 1902, is the city's oldest surviving skyscraper.

The first steel-framed building in London was the Ritz Hotel, built in 1904 and clad in Portland stone. In 1909, the Concrete Institute was incorporated and

The Wills Memorial Tower, Bristol. Photo: Stephen Morris

The Fuller Building, better known as the Flatiron: New York's oldest surviving skyscaper

renamed the Institution of Structural Engineers in 1922. Asbestos, the mined fibrous mineral, was used since the start of the century because of its insulating and fireproof properties. During the subsequent decades, inhalation of its dust was to cause thousands of fatalities but the unrecognised latent period of illness meant that asbestos continued to be generally used until the mid-1980s.

Growth and greed

Until the First World War, about 90 per cent of housing had been privately rented. Post-war, the middle classes no longer needed large houses to accommodate live-in servants and were willing to buy more modest homes. Electric power became generally available and the blossoming motor industry encouraged construction firms to widen their geographical market by utilising lorries to deliver on-site materials. The Building Research Station was established in 1921 to advance efficiency and economy. Experiments were tried to build houses fast with mass-produced components and prefabricated sections and without trained craftsmen. The station amalgamated in 1972 into the Building Research Establishment, which has 'a mission to champion excellence and innovation in the built environment.' (The term 'built environment' was not widely recognised until the 1980s)

Despite the 1929 Wall Street crash and the inter-wars recession, contractors thrived in the housing market. The number of owner-occupied houses grew steadily in response to social trends which discouraged private landlords. About four million homes were built between the wars, bringing the total to 12 million, and far more were built by private enterprise than by local authorities. During the 1930s, Costain, New Ideal Homesteads, Taylor Woodrow and Wimpey became publicly quoted companies. Property developers bought up agricultural land at low cost for 'land bank' investment. Speculative builders, funded by banks or their previous profits and without planning restrictions, concentrated on suburban sprawl and 'ribbon development' along main roads. Ian Nairn, the architectural critic, coined the phrase 'subtopia' in a protest at the bland uniformity destroying the distinction between town and country.

The quality of design and construction generally deteriorated. Most builders considered the time and expense of architects to be unnecessary. 'In the years immediately preceding World War II, the traditional profession of architecture in Europe and in

America was still largely an elitist pursuit: architects designed and built houses for the rich, and grand palaces for corporations and for governments,' wrote Peter Blake (*No Place Like Utopia: Modern Architecture and the Company We Kept*, Norton 1993). Standardised 'pattern-book' houses were often badly built, thermal insulation was unknown, and few had garages because car ownership was rare. John Betjeman complained (*Edwardian England*, Oxford University Press 1964) that builders 'lined their pockets so well from the hideous private housing estates that have appeared since 1920.'

Although architects were employed for social housing developments, the local authorities' policy was one of mundane uniform design. 'The English are a rural-minded people on the whole, which perhaps explains why our rural domestic architecture is so much better than our urban,' wrote Vita Sackville-West in 1941 (*English Country Houses*, Collins). 'Our cities, generally speaking, are deplorable. There is a lack of design which must make the French smile. When the French hint delicately at this we are apt to murmur 'Bath,' and then come to a full stop.'

Why not live at Sudbury Hill?
Small, modern, labour-saving houses with garages and gardens. Live in the country where you will have room to breathe. 40 minutes to Charing Cross. 50 minutes to Mansion House.

		1 Month	3 Months
SEASONS	Charing Cross . .	24/6	67/6
	Mansion House .	26/6	72/6

UNDERGROUND

Developments were also replacing old buildings. 'At the end of the nineteenth century…important Georgian buildings were being demolished wholesale, and after World War I the pace of demolition actually quickened,' wrote Steven Parissien (*The Georgian House*, Aurum Press 1995). The Georgian Group was formed in 1937 'pledged to fight against the tide of demolition.' Parissien stated that the group 'faced an uphill struggle against numerous vested interests and considerable official philistinism.' Crippling death duties were a factor in causing hundreds of country houses to be destroyed. 'Fine houses were sold for their marble chimneypieces and the lead on their roofs,' wrote Robin Fedden in his history of the National Trust (*The Continuing Purpose*, Longmans 1968). 'Timber merchants in a week mercilessly denuded parks which had taken two centuries to mature. The shadow of the demolition contractor fell across the countryside. A national asset, unique and irreplaceable, was wasting.'

Modern Movement

One of the few admired British architects in the mid-twentieth century was Giles Gilbert Scott, designer of the red telephone box, one of the country's most iconic symbols. He designed the New Bodleian Library in Oxford, the University Library at Cambridge, the monumental brick slabs of Liverpool Anglican cathedral and the power stations of Battersea and Bankside in London. (Bankside, built in 1937, was converted by the Swiss architects Jacques Herzog and Pierre de Meuron into Tate Modern, which opened in 2000 and instantly proved to be one of the most successful regenerations of a defunct building.)

Scott was not a follower of the Modern Movement, which rejected Victorian and Edwardian ornateness and introduced new building techniques and plate glass. The movement was initiated abroad rather than in Britain, with Walter Gropius the instigator of the Bauhaus school of design. Founded at Weimar in 1919, Bauhaus exerted an international influence until, in 1933, pressure from the fascist regime forced its closure. Among the refugees to the UK were the Modernist architects Erich Mendelsohn and Serge Chermayeff, who together designed the De La Warr Pavilion on the seafront at Bexhill, East Sussex. It was regarded as the first major steel-frame building in Britain.

Other leading advocates of the Modern Movement who came to Britain were Berthold Lubetkin, born in Russia, and Erno Goldfinger, born in Hungary. The movement in continental Europe championed high-density social apartment blocks, while the British low-density suburban housing was a poor pastiche of the early garden cities. Lubetkin's practice Tecton designed the Highpoint One apartments in Highgate, London, which were intended to be social housing for Gestetner workers. Instead, the 64 apartments were occupied by middle-class tenants. The seven-storey double-cruciform block was inspired by the Swiss architect Le Corbusier's Plan Voisin, meant to be a contemporary town in Paris but never enacted. Le Corbusier's purist ideas to simplify design and dispense with

Modernist Britain: the De La Warr Pavilion, Bexhill, East Sussex, Erich Mendelson and Serge Chermayeff, 1935.

Bankside Power
Station, now
Tate Modern.

ornamentation were advocated in his book
Vers Une Architecture (1923), famously
declaring 'A house is a machine for living.'
Osbert Lancaster, in his book *Homes Sweet
Homes* (John Murray 1939) caustically
commented on 'vast areas of plate-glass'
and the 'rigid and puritanical
functionalism of the Modern Movement.'

Another Modernist house was High
Cross in Devon (*see* page 96), designed in
1932 by William Lescaze, who was born in
Geneva but emigrated to the US. It was
commissioned by Dartington Hall Trust as
the home for the headmaster of Dartington School. Lescaze jointly formed the
partnership of Howe & Lescaze which, in
1932, completed the Philadelphia Saving
Fund Society building. This has been
regarded as the first modern skyscraper

Siemenstadt
Housing, Berlin.
Walter Gropius,
1930.
[*C20th Architecture,*
Jonathan Glancey,
Carlton, 1998]

Highpoint 1, Highgate, London Berthold Lubetkin/Tecton's first major venture into housing in 1935. It came close to realising Le Corbusier's dream for ideal modern cities of gracious flats with balconies overlooking magnificent views across urban parkland.
[*C20th Architecture*, Jonathan Glancey, Carlton, 1998]

because it was not clad in brick or stone but in metal and glass. In New York, 'landmark' buildings included the Art Deco skyscraper Chrysler, designed by William Van Alen and completed in 1930, and the 102-floor Empire State, then the tallest building in the world at 1,472ft (448m). It was finished the following year by the architectural firm Shreve Lamb & Harmon.

In England, an innovative industrial building in the 1930s was the Boots factory at Beeston, Nottingham, designed by the structural engineer Owen Williams and described by the company as 'revolutionary in both design and efficiency.' An admired factory of that period is the former Hoover plant in West London, designed in the Art Deco style by Wallis Gilbert & Partners. It was not, though, praised by the architectural historian Nikolaus Pevsner, who described it as 'perhaps the most offensive of the modernistic atrocities.' Its style was modified for suburban houses in white rendering, green or blue pantiled roofs, and curved windows intended to catch the most sunlight. The design was entertainingly termed 'Hollywood Moderne'.

Post-war plans

Although London suffered serious destruction during the wartime Blitz, so too did many other cities. The roll-call of bomb damage included Birmingham, Bristol, Cardiff, Coventry, Liverpool, Plymouth and Southampton. Tens of thousands of people were killed and some 200,000 homes destroyed. Winston Churchill, the prime minister, arrived in Bristol immediately after a German night raid in 1941. 'The Air Raid Services were feverishly at work and people were still being dug out of the ruins,' he wrote. 'The ordeal had been severe, but the spirit of the citizens was invincible.'

In 1944, when the Education Act brought in the first national system of secondary education, Patrick Abercrombie's Greater London Plan recommended a ring of 'satellite' new towns to relieve London's housing shortage caused by the bombing and overcrowding. A royal commission led to the 1946 New Towns Act. The next year, the Town & Country Planning Act required housing schemes to gain planning permission and to stop ribbon development. Green Belts were mapped to protect countryside from urban encroachment. However, more than 3,000 acres of agricultural land were taken when Stevenage, 30 miles north of London, was designated as the first new town. Lewis Silkin, then Minister for Town & Country Planning, proclaimed: 'Stevenage will, in a short time, become world famous. People from all over the world will come to Stevenage to see how we here in this country are building for the new way of life.'

People were rather more likely to visit the Festival of Britain which, opening on London's South Bank in May 1951, marked the centenary of the Great Exhibition. Its venues, co-ordinated by the architect Hugh Casson, drew 8.5 million visitors during its five months. The centrepiece was the Royal Festival Hall, designed by London County Council architects in a Modernist style to counter the Stalinist classicism of many modern public buildings in continental Europe. The buildings, of which only the Festival Hall survives, brought the Modern Movement into public policy with simple clear forms. Denys Lasdun designed a 15-storey cluster block of flats, Keeling House in Bethnal Green, and Modernism was also demonstrated by the landscaped Alton estates in Roehampton designed by London County Council architects. The style later became known as Brutalism – a word derived from the French beton brut, or rough concrete, but a suitable description of the angular slabs of

Boots factory, Beeston Nottingham, designed by Owen Williams in the 1930s: 'revolutionary in design and efficiency'.

Royal Festival Hall, 1951: the Modern Movement on London's South Bank. [*A Tonic for the Nation*, 1976]

Royal Festival Hall

Le Corbusier's Unité d'habitation in Marseilles, its 17-storey 'vertical village' for communal living completed in 1952. In the wet British climate, flat roofs on houses were to be a mistake and the use of sub-standard cement led to crumbling 'concrete cancer'.

During the grim period of post-war austerity, the Festival was intended to inspire national optimism by promoting arts, science and industry. The Conservatives defeated the Labour government that October by advocating less state control and more individual freedom. The following year, in December 1952, dense 'smog' in London was caused by coal-burning household fires. It brought transport almost to a halt while bronchitis and pneumonia resulted in an estimated 4,000 premature deaths. In eventual response, the first Clean Air Act was introduced in 1956 to require smokeless zones.

Loss of the vernacular

In addition to Stevenage, the government designated new towns run by development corporations, and of which eight were satellites around London. Although the government regarded these schemes to be among the UK's most significant planning achievements, there was elsewhere a minimal control of the scale and quality of development. The pressure of housing shortage allowed exploitation by slum landlords, notoriously Peter Rachman who, in the late 1950s and early 1960s, violently evicted tenants in London to re-let properties at extortionate rents. The National House Building Council, set up just before the Second World War, tried to raise construction standards but was ineffective. Properties were listed from 1950 for historic or architectural merit but aesthetic appreciation was much ignored. Many buildings were demolished – and not only those damaged by wartime bombing or for slum clearance – to make way for concrete shopping centres, multi-lane ring roads and council high-rise blocks. City authorities also moved tenants out of the inner cities to peripheral housing estates. Bristol planners created a monocultural Hartcliffe suburb in the 1950s.

Residential estates like Hartcliffe were built without even a nod towards the vernacular style. Traditional local materials were abandoned while centralised plants produced machine-made bricks, plastic cladding and reconstituted stone. Rural villages and market towns lost much of their character. Orange sodium streetlights caused glaring urbanisation and light pollution. Conservation areas, 'of special architectural or historic interest, the character or appearance of which it is desirable to preserve or enhance,' were not introduced until the Civic Amenities Act in 1967.

Lax official policy failed to apply fiscal measures to protect the countryside by prioritising 'brownfield' rather than 'greenfield' development. Derelict urban sites, often contaminated because of town gas production or industrial processes, discouraged property developers who wanted to make quick profits. Developments were made edge-of-

The Alton estates at Roehampton: a demonstration of high-rise public housing.
[*Architecture in Britain Today*, Michael Webb 1969]

town or out-of-town on what had been farmland. Car-owning and house-buying middle classes quit the despoiled, rundown centres. The inevitable result was damage to the local environment, worsened by a constant rise in commuter traffic.

Obstructive bureaucracy

Property developers and architects who did wish to create imaginative schemes were obstructed by bureaucratic planning and highway regulations. The architect Basil Spence once commented: 'Every young architect knows that the best way to get over the planning committee hurdle is to do a mediocre design that is completely commonplace, and therefore up to the average lay committee's level of appreciation, and he will get it accepted first go.' Building societies were reluctant to advance mortgages on novel designs. Developers were able to cut costs by not needing to commission architects. Instead, they built shoebox houses with no appreciation of local character or tradition. In consequence, much the country's notoriously 'bad architecture' was not, in fact, designed by architects.

Poundbury, Dorchester, Dorset: Prince Charles's vision of a more vernacular Britain.

When there were commissions, disagreements between architect and contractor frequently resulted in delays and cost escalation. Class distinctions still existed within the industry and few students in further or higher education considered construction, rather than architecture or surveying, to be a worthwhile career. The Construction Industry Training Board was not set up until 1964. Labourers would be hired and fired in the same cavalier manner as in the nineteenth century. Inadequate briefing by those commissioning buildings, combined with skills shortages and pressure to reduce costs, resulted in nondescript designs and ill-managed construction, over-spend and dissatisfaction. Often there was no scope for debate on design and materials, as these had been already written into the drawings, specifications and bill of quantities. Almost invariably, a client would choose the lowest-priced tender.

High rise, low quality

Techniques of prefabrication, with the use of precast concrete, had long been used for civil engineering projects and wartime defences. Post-war, the government and local authorities promoted industrialised building for schools and social housing as a quick, cheap method of construction. Over 7,000 schools, partially prefabricated, were built in the two decades after the war, while the government and councils decided that prefabricated apartments and tower blocks were the simplest solution to meet housing demand. It was presumed that inner-city high-storey flats could also lessen property expansion within Green Belts. The 1956 Housing Act gave councils even more incentives by introducing subsidies for every floor built over five storeys.

Although high-rise buildings were assumed to be symbols of the Modern Movement, it was engineers rather than architects who were mostly responsible for their construction. Many towers were not only ugly buildings on windswept estates, with white concrete soon stained, but were to result in long-term, costly problems such as poor heating and ventilation, inadequate insulation and damaging water penetration. 'It was considered essential to complete as many homes as possible,' stated the authors Roger C. Harvey and Allan Ashworth in *The Construction Industry of Gt Britain* (Newnes 1993). 'Government, and opportunistic contractors, used their influence in order to ensure that local authority housing departments recognised that industrialised building was ideal for the rapid production of multi-storey flats. Unfortunately, during this period and subsequent decades, industrialised building contributed to a number of spectacular failures.' The most spectacular was to be Ronan Point in East London, a system-built block of council flats. A gas cooker's explosion, on the eighteenth floor, caused several fatalities as one side of the building collapsed.

Popular disapproval of modern buildings was shared by Prince Charles in his book *A Vision of Britain: A personal view of architecture* (Doubleday 1989): 'The fashionable architectural themes of the 1950s and 1960s…have spawned deformed monsters which have come to haunt our towns and cities, our villages and our countryside…If we deny the architectural past – and the lessons to be learnt from our ancestors – then our buildings also lose their souls. If we abandon the traditional principles upon which architecture was based for 2,500 years or more, then our civilisation suffers.'

Britain's economy improved, though, and Harold Macmillan's electoral slogan 'You've never had it so good' kept the Tories in power in 1959. But people did not regard architects and builders as being so good. In 1961, a government inquiry chaired by Parker Morris produced a report *Homes for Today and Tomorrow*. It sought to improve the much-needed quality of social housing, recommending standards which included minimum room spaces and heating systems. Councils gradually adopted the standards – although the mandatory standards were abolished by the Conservative government in 1980 – and there was some influence upon the private sector. It was during the year the report was published that two young men, John Pontin and Tim Organ, started a construction company in Bristol. They were to be pioneers in rejuvenating a forgotten concept from the pre-Victorian days: design and build. The company was to become JT Group.

3 A concept reborn
John Pontin and Tim Organ create the business

Every building creates associations in the mind of the beholder
Nikolaus Pevsner (1902-1983)

At the start of the 1960s, the inefficient and adversarial state of the construction industry was frustratingly apparent to John Pontin and Tim Organ, who were colleagues working for the Bristol subsidiary of a national contractor. While they believed they could rise to senior positions in the company, neither wanted that particular career path.

John Pontin, born in June 1937 and one of three children of a postman, had been brought up in Southville, Bristol, a working-class district of the inner city close to the docks. During his childhood, he suffered from pleurisy, with 10 months spent in a sanatorium. He went to the local primary school where in 1947 he was placed 38th out of a class of 45 pupils. The head teacher wrote a report: 'John could do better – he does not concentrate.' After failing his 11-plus exam, John went to learn at Bristol Technical School's building department. It was there that he became interested in design and would have wished to train as an architect. However, having been unable to attend grammar school, he lacked the academic qualifications.

Instead, when aged 16, John joined the building firm of John Knox, the Bristol subsidiary of Bryant Contractors, based in Birmingham. For the first year, John had the clerical job of organising pay packets, making tea and answering phones. He was promoted into the drawing office and then became a junior building surveyor, attending day release and evening classes. At the age of 18, because of his childhood pleurisy, he was assessed as unfit for National Service. In 1958, John gained a higher national diploma and won the annual South-west England quantity surveying award. He recalled it as a 'magic year, with everything becoming good,' and it gave him the self-confidence to be highly ambitious.

The same year, Tim Organ, the son of an architect and a year older than John, joined John Knox. Tim had been brought up in Weston-super-Mare and, like John, his school education had not been high-flying – he too failed his 11-plus exam – and he was much more interested in sport. When he left school, a friend lent him a collection of *The Builder* magazine (launched in 1842, it was renamed *Building* in 1966) and it spurred him to become interested in construction. As a conscientious objector to National Service, he was employed instead for two years in building work and achieved a higher national diploma in a sandwich course, studying at Bristol College of Technology. He worked briefly for a building firm in Weston-super-Mare before joining John Knox as an assistant site manager, working on an extension of Fry's huge chocolate factory at Keynsham, near Bristol.

Two shared ideas

Bryant, the firm's parent company, decided that John Knox must have a contract planning department and John was transferred to run that small department in Bedminster, Bristol. Tim, after his work on Fry's factory extension, was transferred to that office. 'We were producing plans – critical path networks and gant charts – and trying to persuade the site managers that there was a tool they could use to run their projects,' Tim said. 'That was hard work, and out of that frustration grew the idea that if there was any merit in integrating design and production, we ought to go ahead and do it.'

Both John and Tim enrolled at Bristol Polytechnic for an Institute of Management two-year course. 'It was as though scales were falling off my eyes,' Tim recalled. 'We talked about marketing, human relationships – industrial psychology they called it at that time – value engineering and accountancy. It was just amazing to look at the organisation of work not through a builder's eyes but through the wider spectrum of management. John also got incredibly interested in these lectures and we went to a lecture almost every night.

'I think that made us realise what a ridiculous industry we were working in, where builders made their money, or a lot of them did, through adversarial management. It was obvious that, if you could only harness all of the resources in the industry, there was a huge opportunity. What John and I were pursuing was a very old-fashioned idea. Bath, for example, had been constructed through design and build by master builders.

'To his credit, John tried very hard to get Bryant to pursue this as a way of developing the company. The difficulty was in changing a large organisation which had established ways of working. It would be like getting a tanker to change directions – you could only do it very slowly. And of course we were both ambitious and full of enthusiasm and wanted to get on and do something.'

Planning the business

By this time, at the start of the 1960s, post-war austerity was dissipating and social attitudes were changing apace. Commercial television had begun and the public was influenced by consumer advertising, glossy magazines and Hollywood films glamorising the American way of life. As wages rose, people had money to spend on fashionable clothes, televisions, refrigerators, record players and cars. The Mini car, designed by Alec Issigonis and launched in 1959, became an icon of what was to be depicted as the 'Swinging Sixties'. Britain's higher education responded to social changes with the expansion of polytechnics and universities. Sussex University was opened in 1960 on its green campus with Basil

Young
entrepreneurs:
Tim Organ and
John Pontin on
the Rackhay roof.

Spence's red-brick architecture. The University of East Anglia was founded in 1961, also on a parkland campus, with Denys Lasdun's ziggurat-style halls of residence.

Despite the social transformation, the construction industry perpetuated its old attitudes. No 'grand vision' was being promoted to reform the industry. John and Tim became increasingly dissatisfied with their role in the Bryant subsidiary. John remembered Tim saying, 'If we can't do better than this, we need shooting.' Tim recalled: 'We'd become friends, kindred spirits, although with different backgrounds. We talked about the future and I can't say whose idea it was to set up our company. But it was almost all born out of frustration and very much a joint decision.' Both became convinced that, with their employers being reluctant to adopt new methods, they should seek to be entrepreneurs starting a business from scratch. They visualised that, by setting up a company which integrated design with construction, they could offer package deals to clients in a co-operative, rather than adversarial, manner. In that way, their own careers could be more rewarding and enjoyable.

'I think, in fact, it was more difficult for John – clearly he was destined to become a director of Bryant,' said Tim. 'He had a secure route through to the top. He was very highly regarded by Bryant themselves – they wanted to keep him. I didn't have any sort of allegiance – I wasn't embedded in the organisation. I was more wedded to the idea of pursuing what I had learnt and the development of my ideas than in pursuing a career with any one company.'

Neither John nor Tim, who was married with a baby son, had the financial resources to make it easy to establish a company. While still working for John Knox in 1960, they urged a senior surveyor in the firm to join them in setting up their proposed business. The surveyor declined but suggested they could tender for the extension of Pratts Garage, which was owned by the surveyor's uncle at Westbury-on-Trym in north Bristol. They quoted £3,000 for the five repair bays which the garage required. Its owner was so satisfied with the modest tender price that he asked them to construct seven bays for £4,500.

Company start-up

John and Tim stayed with John Knox until they received their Christmas bonus in December 1960, for which they each received £100. With that capital, they resigned and were ordered to quit immediately. They set up their business in a first-floor bedroom in Tim's rented Victorian terraced house in Coronation Road, Bristol, close to John's childhood home. They equipped the business with a phone, a van and a ladder and named the firm JT (Bristol) Ltd after the initials of their forenames. Roger Mortimer, who was later to be its first company architect, wrote in a review of JT's early history that the use of their first-name initials 'typified the youthful informality, enthusiasm and optimism of John and Tim's approach. These qualities, combined with a hard-working, hands-on approach, attracted loyal staff from the outset.'

On February 2, 1961, John and Tim – aged 23 and 24 respectively – gained planning consent for the Pratts Garage extension. It was a memorable date in the company's history, effectively the opening day of the business. John, who was living in Fishponds, Bristol, persuaded fellow players of the local Trinity Athletic football club to volunteer to prepare the garage site with demolition work over the weekend. 'I started digging the foundations myself by hand,' Tim remembered, 'and by the end of the first week we poured the concrete into the foundations, drew our first cheque, and we were in business. The following Monday we employed our first two bricklayers and a labourer.'

Monthly payments to builders were the industry's usual practice but JT initiated a different form of contract which clients would be willing to accept. 'We would not wait to be paid until a month's work had been done,' John said. 'We received payments when we reached each stage – at the end of the foundations stage, 10 per cent of the contract; up to first floor, another 15 per cent; and so on.' This could result in almost weekly payments and, as materials were paid for on a monthly basis, JT benefited from the cash flow. 'This caused us to want to build fast and expeditiously. That was extraordinarily helpful to us during the early years.'

The next projects that summer were in Bristol – a chalet-style house for £2,500 and a clubhouse for Redland Lawn Tennis Club. The clubhouse, with a lounge, bar, showers and changing rooms, was completed within just five weeks after planning consent. The next project was subcontracted to JT by Bert Wells, a general housebuilder. Wells was chairman of a youth club in Fishponds and John, when a 19-year-old club member, had been asked to volunteer to design and help build an aluminium-roofed building for the club. As John recalled, 'He eventually knew that we were in business and he subcontracted the houses to us about six months after we started.'

As their fledgling business grew that year, domestic inflation rose and wage rates escalated in response to labour shortages. International political tensions heightened in the 'Cold War' as the East German Communists built the Berlin Wall. In the autumn, the economy began to improve, with a recovery in the balance of payments and a strengthening pound. By the end of its first year, JT's turnover reached £51,300 with John and Tim able to pay themselves about £1,000 each, a similar amount paid to individual craftsmen. During 1962, the company completed on schedule the Shirehampton Golf Clubhouse near Avonmouth and it soon had about 30 employees although, in common with other building firms, it suffered from post-war shortages of materials and labour skills. Roger Mortimer, in his review, commented: 'The loyalty and flexibility of the small group of key operatives was critical in the first year or two, as directly employed labour was the norm. Some of these staff stayed to become site managers. But JT's construction approach was soon based on sub-contracting, little developed at that time. This, together with close and mutually beneficial relations with suppliers, helped to get jobs finished to timetables and at cost levels which surprised and gratified the clients.'

Despite the company's fast expansion, John and Tim had yet to evolve the business beyond the 'pattern-book' methods. 'We had the idea of uniting design and production,' Tim stated, 'but I don't think we had at that time any fantastic architectural aspirations. We certainly wanted to produce some good architecture, but I think we were initially very successful at designing buildings that could be constructed incredibly quickly by current industry standards.'

New York: new ideas

In April 1962, almost by serendipity, John and Tim were to find innovative ways to marry design with construction. The two partners heard that there was to be a building studies trip, organised in Bristol, to visit New York. Tim's family commitments prevented him from travelling and instead John went, a solitary young builder on a flight with over 100 architects. The group was to see New York's startling architecture, which included two recently-completed landmark buildings: the 38-storey bronze-clad, brown-tinted glass Seagram Building, designed by Ludwig Mies van der Rohe, and the white organic spiral of Frank Lloyd Wright's Guggenheim museum.

During a free morning for the tour group, John was walking alone on the rainswept streets of Manhattan. Noticing the plaque of Uris Inc, described as a real estate company, he walked into the plush reception area, mainly to get out of the rain, and introduced himself as a builder from England. To his surprise, he was invited by its chief executive to meet for lunch in a restaurant. John was told about Uris's specialism in designing and constructing major steel-framed buildings. The 2,200-room New York Hilton Hotel was being built by the company at that time, to be completed in only 18 months. 'It was just good luck to meet him – it was like meeting a friend, he was so instructive and so helpful,' John recalled. 'It was two hours' worth of extreme generosity on his part.'

Uris was not alone in the United States in reviving the pre-Victorian concept of design and build. The Austin Company, founded in 1878 in Ohio, claimed that as early as 1904 Wilbert J. Austin 'conceived the then heretical idea of combining engineering and construction in one firm to offer a complete facility service. This concept, which later became known as the Austin Method, broadened the traditional approach to construction by offering contracts that started with architecture and engineering, and ended with the finished building.' Other American companies were to adopt the principle of design and build. Opus Corporation, based in Minneapolis, was founded in 1953 by Gerry Rauenhorst and claimed to be a pioneer. A member of the Design-Build Institute of America, it declared: 'Development, architecture and engineering, construction, and property management all come together under one, single-source process. That is the Opus philosophy that has created award-winning buildings and properties.'

The concept of design and build was fresh to Britain. IDC of Stratford-upon-Avon, in the early 1960s, started to specialise in the design and construction of industrial buildings. (It was acquired in 1985 by Matthew Hall Group which itself was brought into AMEC in 1988) Shepherd Building Group, based in York, began in 1962 to integrate design and build as a procurement route – a 'procurement route' is defined as the organisational structure accepted by a client for the management of the planning, design and construction of a building. The company, founded by Frederick Shepherd in the late nineteenth century, became one of Europe's largest privately owned businesses in the engineering and construction industry.

'I remember John coming back from New York full of ideas. It was an exciting opportunity,' Tim recalled. Together, they envisaged the way in which JT could advance the 'package deal' concept of design and build for all kinds of buildings, however sophisticated. By employing in-house architects, the company could control a project from start to finish, eliminating the habitual three-way wrangles between client, architect and contractor. Delays and costs would be reduced, enabling the business to offer competitive and lucrative tenders. The concept, the two partners decided, was to be put into practice – including a subsidiary to erect concrete frames with the name Uris, as a tribute to John's inspirational Manhattan meeting.

4 The breakthrough:
JT takes a leading role

It is enterprise which builds and improves the world's possessions
John Maynard Keynes (1883-1946)

Soon after John Pontin's American visit, JT won its biggest project yet, a seven-storey block of 13 flats called Harley Court in Clifton, Bristol. In August 1962, a sales representative from a steel-rod engineering supplier had made an unsolicited call on JT, which was still based in Tim's upstairs bedroom. John said: 'He asked if we wanted any steel-rod reinforcement and we regaled him with the idea of the New York concept which we wanted to promote. He said he knew of a client and this led us on to Harley Court.'

David and Joyce Perry were planning the flats with Roger Mortimer, a partner of the architectural practice Alexander Beckingsale & Partners. JT got in touch with Roger who asked if the firm wanted to quote for the building's box-frame structure. It quoted £20,000 and was then invited to tender for the whole building. The bid was accepted at £105,000 and the Perrys agreed to pay money promptly each month, the cash flow making it possible for JT to manage the contract. 'It was a really big breakthrough,' John recalled. After 18 months in Tim's house in Coronation Road, they moved to Hill Street, Kingswood, and also rented an office in Small Street, in Bristol's city centre. Two friends asked JT to convert the Small Street ground floor as a restaurant, the Cornucopia, and to put a trattoria in the basement. These were run in a 50 per cent financial partnership with the friends as restaurateurs.

Work on Harley Court began in December 1962. Despite the harsh snowy winter, the coldest of many years, Harley Court was built under a fast programme with many decisions made at site meetings. 'It was an interesting experience and frightening at times,' Roger remembered, 'but I greatly enjoyed contacts with John and Tim, the first builders I knew on first-name terms.' Roger was then commissioned for eight townhouses in Shirehampton, Bristol, which were commended for good design by the Ministry of Housing and Local Government, the first of JT's design awards.

Conflict culture

During 1963, the year was of highly eventful matters. The US was involved in the Vietnam war and the British government's application to join the European Economic Community was vetoed by France's president Charles de Gaulle. A worsening financial position of the railways caused the government to commission a report by Dr Richard Beeching to establish a viable network. *The Re-Shaping of British Railways* – called the Beeching Report – caused an immense upheaval in the transport system. Car ownership was escalating and the government used the report to justify the motorway building programme. It closed more than 2,000 stations and about a quarter of the rail network. Harold Macmillan, after the John Profumo affair, resigned as prime minister in October and was succeeded by Alec Douglas-Home. That November, John F. Kennedy was assassinated.

Inflation and slow growth continued to affect the British economy and in 1964 the Conservative government was defeated by the Labour Party, led by Harold Wilson. During that year, a government inquiry was held into the 'conflict culture' of the construction industry, for which the public sector was the main client. The inquiry's findings, known as the Banwell Report, identified the separation of design and construction as a major cause of the industry's poor performance. The report advocated selective rather than open tendering, and serial tendering which could offer benefits for both client and contractor (*Placing and Management of Contracts for Building and Civil Engineering Works, Ministry of Public Buildings and Works*, 1964.)

Two decades before, in 1944, the Simon Committee report (T*he Placing and Management of Building Contracts*, HMSO) had condemned the traditional method where, in the selection of a main contractor, the emphasis was placed on the lowest price tender. There was poor workmanship because many builders were unscrupulous in cutting costs. This study was largely ignored. Other studies tried to reinforce the view that the structure of the industry had to be reformed. Marian Bowley, author of *Innovation in Building Materials* (Gerald Duckworth, 1960) had explained why innovation was retarded. Studies by the Tavistock Institute (*Communications in the Building Industry*, 1965 and *Interdependence and Uncertainty: A Study of the Building Industry*, 1966) considered that there was a need for greater client focus, with the industry's separate loyalties being the main problem to overcome. The Tavistock Institute's reference to communications greatly influenced John and Tim. It was the focus of much company training in the early years and good, often informal, communications were a key feature of JT's design and build success.

Overall, the construction industry remained complacent, unlike the motor and aerospace industries which were being restructured. Inadequate training, aversion to risk and a defensive attitude meant most companies continued to show little enthusiasm for 'best practice'. Instead, JT had already adopted 'revolutionary thinking,' Roger Mortimer noted. 'JT was early to recognise that building is a service industry and that satisfied clients are fundamental to staying in business. The inability of builders to control or even influence designers was seen as an important cause of the industry's poor reputation.'

Harley Court, Clifton. Photo: Stephen Morris

The business grows

JT itself was growing at an exponential rate. In autumn 1964, its board commissioned consultants, Urwick, Orr & Partners, to 'identify the problems arising from very rapid expansion over the past two to three years' and to advise on the most appropriate solutions. The consultants reported: 'The sales turnover of the group is now running at approximately £450,000 a year, and you have doubled the turnover each year since the first company was founded in 1961. You estimate that in the next few years you can achieve a group turnover of £1m, and your aim is to become a public company within ten years.' (That aim – to be a quoted company – was never to be pursued.)

Urwick, Orr was concerned that the majority of staff were new to the company and the liquid cash position was not healthy. 'There is no doubt that your accounts section requires a major overhaul with the object of producing essential management control information lacking at present...Your rapid growth has not only produced strains in your financial position and accounting, but your organisation also displays symptoms of too fast a growth.' It said it was vital for JT to tidy up its administration, to develop operating procedures including the strengthening of the link between design, quantity surveying and planning, and to ensure that its new staff had a sound knowledge of their duties with an appropriate training programme. JT, it emphasised, should have a planned rate of growth.

'We freely acknowledge the outstanding performance on your part in building the group to its present size in the space of 2/3 years,' the consultants told John and Tim. 'This rapid growth has demanded hard work, imagination and drive, and there is no doubt you, as the founder-directors, have demonstrated these qualities.'

Company architect

Roger Mortimer felt 'flattered but doubtful' when asked to join JT and he took six months of persuasion, and then had to give six months' notice. Although JT had commissioned outside architects to help with its package deal contracts, mostly in housing, the two partners decided that in-house design was essential if the design and build concept were to be fully exploited. 'David Perry was a very successful developer who gave us more and more work,' said Tim, 'and somehow John persuaded Roger to leave the architectural practice to join us. We didn't want just to produce buildings – we wanted to produce architecture.' Roger had trained at college in Bournemouth and the Royal West of England Academy's school of architecture, qualifying in 1953. After National Service in the Royal Engineers, he worked in the architectural department of British Aircraft Corporation at Filton, Bristol. The professions were in-house and almost all work was negotiated with only one or two builders whose advice was welcomed. To a limited extent, it was a precursor of design and build. But the department closed and Roger was made redundant. He joined Alexander

Beckingsale & Partners where, after a couple of years, he became a partner for the next five years.

At the age of 33, he joined JT in 1965 as company architect and, when he became a director in 1969, he had to resign from the RIBA. Fellow professionals showed surprise at his decision to join JT and some architects were hostile. They feared that their own practices might be threatened by a business which integrated architectural design with construction. Roger himself considered he was on a 'major learning curve' in joining JT. 'I really had little feel then for design and build and only moved because of the challenge and my enjoyment of working with John and Tim,' he remembered. 'It was the style, personality and sheer enthusiasm of the founders that persuaded me and others to leave good jobs for JT. This, combined with the promise of a more interesting and productive career, continued to be a vital recruitment tool as we grew. JT were not known for paying high salaries!

'I had immediately some exciting design opportunities and the opportunity to develop my interest in modern architecture – for example, with a church – and saw jobs rapidly go on site. Within weeks, I had no doubts about my move and was involved in matters well beyond conventional architects' work.' The church, on a restricted site in Fishponds, Bristol, was a merger of two Methodist chapels which wanted to combine their congregations. The £40,000 project to design, build and fit out the church, together with a hall, was completed within the contract period. It was, JT reported, 'done with even the flower vases in the contract price and a profit was made.'

Roger recalled: 'Both Tim and John were very interested in architecture in itself, but particularly as an important opportunity in its impact on cost, speed and ease of construction and, of course, profit. Only speedy, efficient and therefore profitable turnover would enable survival. I appreciated this reluctance to waste materials – my upbringing in the post-war 'utility' world perhaps influenced me. Now I was in an environment where people knew what materials cost, and I learned to use informed comment on buildability and cost aspects.' JT's two founders showed their liking for modern design by commissioning Roger to design both of their own new homes in Somerset.

Staff relations

By then, JT had gained a substantial staff, most of them site workers, and with two main companies in the group: JT (Bristol) Ltd, to carry out the construction work with Tim as managing director and based in Hill Street, and Building Partnership (Bristol) Ltd to design buildings with John as managing director and based in Small Street. Two other subsidiaries – Uris, working on concrete frames, and Pylex, which carried out electrical work – were also based in Hill Street, with Tim as their managing director. David Pontin,

John's younger brother, had joined JT in 1964 to be its financial controller. He came from a chartered accountancy firm after his National Service. 'It was undoubtedly good management of the cash flow which enabled JT to grow at the very fast rate that it did,' he commented. 'I was working 12 to 14 hours a day – and I loved it.'

JT's turnover, in the year to October 1965, reached £619,870 with pre-tax profits of £10,570. Des Williams, who had worked with Costain for 10 years, joined JT that year as senior project manager and proved to be a key long-term executive of the business. Tim described him as 'the best building manager I ever worked with.' David Pontin remembered: 'Des was absolutely brilliant and Roger was a kingpin. It was a damn good team.' Ken Greeves came from an architectural private practice to be responsible for the design of industrial and commercial buildings. Andrew Misselbrook joined as quantity surveyor. Des's brother Howard arrived in 1968 as senior project manager, having previously worked with John Laing.

Company Architect: Roger Mortimer, c.1970.

The company, gaining recognition with its design and build policy, raised its status within the industry, attracting more qualified people by offering good career opportunities. The 'team spirit' attitude, in the co-ordination of projects, boosted staff morale. 'If you work only for the money,' Tim commented, 'it steers your life towards a much more consumerist approach to living, whereas I would like to think you get dignity and pleasure from work, or should be able to. I found it exhilarating that we put up buildings so much faster than anyone else. There was this great sense of camaraderie and purpose that was within the company.'

JT did not advocate trade union membership, to avoid the conventional conflict of Bosses versus Workers. The industry had a fragmented structure typified by the variety of trade unions:

Amalgamated Society of Woodworkers

Amalgamated Society of Painters and Decorators

Association of Building Technicians

Amalgamated Union of Building Trade Workers

It was not until 1971 that these unions came together to form the Union of Construction, Allied Trades and Technicians (Ucatt). Very few women, other than secretarial and clerical staff, were employed, then or later. Employers, responding to the highly cyclical nature of the industry, persisted in short-term hiring and firing, ready to sack workers at no notice. If workers fell ill, they were more likely to be dismissed than to be allowed sick leave.

Instead, JT introduced novel labour relations. 'We had a co-partnership committee which met every month and every trade was represented on that committee,' Tim stated. 'Staff could raise any issue they liked in respect of the way the company was moving, the work they were doing, its attitude to men, safety and so on. Our industrial relations were years ahead of the building industry.' The company was later to acquire holiday cottages for the use of employees. (Staff policy included employee shareholdings, profit-sharing and health insurance schemes) 'We had, for example, a sick-pay scheme which we contributed to and the men contributed to, but the money was then given to the men to manage,' he recalled. 'As a consequence, the men were much stricter with themselves than we could have ever been as an employer.

'It was certainly an ambition of ours to have this concern for people,' Tim said. 'That's reflected in the fact that about two thirds of the first 30 employees achieved some sort of management role. The company actively encouraged them to continue to learn and to take courses and to improve their position.'

There were other aspects of staff relations which were rare within the industry. 'We were paying our operatives a flat rate for every hour that they worked on the basis that overtime was bad for them and not very productive for us,' he said. 'So there was no incentive for them to want to work overtime. If it were necessary for us to ask the men to work overtime, we did pay them extra. But if a man wanted to work longer hours to make up his income, it was always on that flat rate of pay.'

The staff were trained to be much more adaptable in their skills than normally within the construction industry. 'We had this idea that, with a flexible workforce, we could involve the men in what we were doing – we could actually design the buildings to suit the skills we had on board,' he said. 'We did recruit some really good guys – whenever we needed somebody, we always sought the advice of the workforce and we hired people through recommendation, not through advertisement.'

Broadening horizons

Nationally, innovation and company mergers accelerated during the 1960s. The mergers created big corporations which eroded regional character as many chain hotels, pubs and shops lost their individuality. Fashion frenzy was inspired by designers such as Mary Quant and Barbara Hulanicki and the boutiques of Kings Road in Chelsea and Carnaby Street in Soho. Terence Conran founded the Habitat chain of stores and the pop music of the Beatles and Rolling Stones revolutionised young culture. In 1966 – the year England hosted and won the football World Cup – the Bristol sub-region and South Wales benefited from a crucial piece of infrastructure: the Severn road bridge across the mile-wide estuary to replace a car ferry. The M4 between London and South Wales was not completed until the early 1970s, when it spawned the 'Thames Valley corridor' of new businesses.

During 1966, national building regulations, enforced by local councils, came into operation to apply structural standards for health and safety. That same year JT built for Greencoat Properties a speculative multi-storey building in Bristol to provide showrooms, offices and warehousing. An unexpected discovery during its site clearance was a plague burial ground. A second development in the city for Greencoat that year was a 25,000 sq ft office block, called Rackhay, in Queen Charlotte Street. JT moved into part of the building from its existing two sites to be its new headquarters, with the rest of the building as lettable offices. Derek Robinson came from John Laing, where he had been in charge of its buying department for Scotland, to be chief buyer supervising the procurement of all materials.

The Rackhay's open-plan offices made it easier for the project teams to work together – the space was unpartitioned and there were no separate departments. The in-house design capability enabled JT to offer sites to developers as realistically costed projects. This was an effective way of winning new business and demonstrating the company's ability to handle large projects. Its growth was also stimulated by the company's determination to forge close relations with its clients. John said: 'The degree of trust that we had to engender with our first contract was, hopefully, with a client who would be interested in repeat business with us – typically, supermarket groups or property developers. The difficulty was in getting that first contract signed and for us to deliver a quality service. Once we got the first contract, it was up to us not to lose the client. We bent over backwards to perform extremely well in order that the second contract or third contract became almost routine. What was the point of winning a new client if one lost an existing one?

'In a way, that explains how we became a regional and national company,' he said. 'Having shown a client what could be done in the Bristol region, if the client was building elsewhere, then why not? It was a mutual relationship whereby we wanted to demonstrate that we were so good, relative to the rest of the competition, that the client would be anxious to keep us in business. We were offering something quite unique and that's the nice relationship that all businesses ought to aspire to. Even if there weren't repeat orders, a developer might give a word of mouth recommendation to another developer. We were supported by clients who wanted us to keep afloat.'

Staff issues were more complex as the company widened its geographical market and took on more recruits. Tim recalled: 'I was told at college – a truism – that the difference between one organisation and another is the people who make it up. That's one of the factors that made JT very special. Designing and building was important because everyone

had a part to play in the project. But John was very keen to develop other aspects of the business. He was pursuing it on a regional if not a national basis by then. The rapid growth of the company did leave some people behind – its expansion outgrew their ability. The nature of the work changed and the place of work changed. John quite rightly was ambitious and industrious in creating more and more opportunities, whereas for me, I was looking at it in a much more parochial, consolidated sort of way. But we didn't fall out over it. We've never fallen out.'

Partnership ends

The troubled British economy resulted in sterling's devaluation in November 1967. The exchange rate was reduced to $2.40, down from $2.80. Harold Wilson, the prime minister, in a much-derided statement, declared: 'It does not mean, of course, that the pound here in Britain, in your pocket or purse or in your bank, has been devalued.' For JT, it was also a time of change. Bovis, the national construction company, proposed taking a substantial stake in the company and JT's board considered accepting it because of its own liquidity problems, suffering then from the cyclical nature of the industry. After some deliberation, the board decided to reject the investment.

JT's original partnership, though, was ending. Tim decided he wanted to take a new direction in his career. He had been always more interested in architecture than actual construction, influenced by his architect father and older brother Robert – an artist who had studied at Slade School of Art and was a painting tutor at Falmouth School of Art. Tim was responsible mainly for housing which was a large tranche of the business. An estate of 25 houses, for example, had been completed at Thornbury, Gloucestershire, in 1965. Nationally, private and council house completions were reaching a post-war annual peak of 352,000. 'We had acquired quite a lot of housing work,' Tim said. 'It was my pigeon but in variance to the way I was hoping the organisation would develop because high-volume housing is very much short-cycle, repetitive work. Whereas, engrained in the JT workforce at that time, there was the notion that we could do everything with a very flexible workforce.

Robert and Tim Organ, Wrington, 1972
Photo: Garth Smith

'So that was a major problem for me,' he said. 'The houses we built were good and we were pushing the market. We had come up with the idea of four-bedroomed houses with a simple spacious plan and economic building cost which was unmatched in the area at the time.' This type of design was the subject of intensive scrutiny by architects, builders and tradesmen to ensure buildability and value for money. The process was enabled by the Institute of Operations Research to which JT had been introduced by the Tavistock Institute. Roger Mortimer recalled that this open questioning of every decision, which might now be called lateral thinking, became an everyday feature of the company's approach. With other techniques such as 'variety reduction' and 'critical path networking", multi-skilled teams were to produce best-value solutions.

Tim, however, considered that 'the more the work moved towards short-cycle repetitive operations, the more the workforce were interested just in the money and not in the quality of what they were actually doing. I was very much into this idea of co-ownership where all the employees were sharing in the profitability of the company. For me, that was the right and best way. But if you start working in a different market place – as in repetitive housing – it did bring about strains because it was less expensive for us not to use our own labour but to sub-contract. As I wasn't enamoured of repetitive housing, and rather than to cause a massive problem for the company, I saw the future as something a little different.' Housing was also not proving to be profitable in contrast to other building work.

He decided to resign to form his own company, Artist Constructor Ltd, together with his brother Robert in 1969. Artist Constructor was to become a long-established business designing individual properties and later to be named Form Structures. John bought Tim out of their equal share ownership with compensation. The end of the partnership was not acrimonious but Tim felt it was the right decision. 'Looking back,' he said, 'I can say that if I had stayed with JT, I could have caused real tensions within the company.'

5 Design and build in practice
Its innovative management

For which of you, intending to build a tower, sitteth not down first, and counteth the cost, whether he have sufficient to finish it? St. Luke, Chapter 14:28.

By 1970, the year when the Conservatives defeated Harold Wilson's Labour government and Edward Heath – the son of a builder – became prime minister, JT had established itself as a design and build company with a broadly-based and experienced management. Emphasising that 'building is a service industry,' it claimed: 'The design and build service, often known as the package deal, has grown rapidly at the expense of the more normal methods of building procurement.'

JT Building Group, named as the new holding company in 1971, remained small compared to the big national construction companies. The first substantial project away from the West of England had been in 1969, the year when Tim Organ resigned. JT built a factory and offices for Bristol Potteries at Camborne in Cornwall, with the managers saving travel time by hiring a light aircraft. The executive team, while responsible for overall policy decisions, were all involved in day to day work. In 1972, the team consisted of John Pontin and Roger Mortimer as directors and six others:

> the architects Stuart Edwards, specialising in major commercial projects, and Ken Greeves, responsible for the design of industrial and commercial buildings (both resigned from the RIBA that year)
> Derek Robinson, chief buyer
> Des and Howard Williams, brothers who were both senior project managers, and
> David Pontin, board secretary concentrating on financial policy.

Nationally, there was perpetual debate by academics, management consultants and government in what way the construction process could be improved to complete buildings in less time for less money and to a higher quality. But the industry had hardly modernised its procedures. Conventional contracts during the 1970s remained much the most common, with the consequences that clients – as ever – had reason to fear the complications.

The procurement strategy should be to identify the best way to achieve the overall objectives of the client's chosen project, taking account of the purpose of the planned building, the forecast time taken for its design and construction, the available budget, and the asset value of the building and its intended lifespan. The client, unless experienced in property matters, would need expert advice. Such advice, though, was often limited and the client's brief might well be inadequate.

Conventional route

The industry's conventional procurement route required the appointment of an architect, who assumed the role of lead consultant, and other professionals such as an engineer and quantity surveyor. The architect was normally chosen by his or her reputation and when already known to the client. With standard fee scales, imposed by the RIBA and based on a percentage of the final cost of the building, there was then no fee competition. The architect would establish the client's requirements and design the building, with possible help by consultants who were also employed directly by the client, and usually subject to advice by a quantity surveyor on the cost. Planning consent was likely to be applied for at this stage. The quantity surveyor then produced the bill of quantities, which involved measuring all the quantities of materials and labour implied by the drawings, on a trade by trade basis. This was the most important contract document.

Many elements were not fully designed at this stage or were uncertain, such as ground conditions and foundations. Work would be re-measured on site to help calculate both interim and final payments to the contractor. Much of the work, such as plumbing and electrical fittings, was specified to be carried out by nominated subcontractors, selected by the client's consultants.

Tenders were then obtained from between three to six contractors – sometimes more – and based on the bill of quantities. The architect's drawings were not a contract document but could be inspected at the architect's office. Price competition was restricted due to the detailed specification of materials and construction, and the large elements that were to be carried out by nominated subcontractors, for which provisional or 'prime cost' sums were specified. The difference between tenders was often due mainly to the contractors' mark-up for overhead and profit. As the industry margins rarely exceeded 3 per cent, it was unsurprising that tenders were often close in price. It was customary to accept the lowest tender, subject to a check by the quantity surveyor on that contractor's priced bill of quantities.

Given these tight margins, contractors would attempt to enhance their profits during the construction period and this inevitably led to claims for additional payments and sometimes destructive negotiations between the builder and client. Any delays or costs caused by conflicting or late drawings generated extra costs to the client. Variations to the scope of work could cause claims for extra contract time and therefore associated overheads. The appointment of major sub-contractors by the architect, rather than the main contractors, might also cause arguments on site.

This traditional approach provided fertile ground for dispute with details which were rarely known to the long-suffering client. The contractors' lack of opportunity to discuss buildability during the design stage would add to cost, time and quality problems. Many contracts were late and, after the long negotiations that often followed site completion, clients were faced with higher costs.

Common problems

Although this contractual process during the 1970s could produce good results which satisfied clients, the cultural and practical divisions between all parties led to common problems. Construction with a commitment to economic, environmental and social sustainability was not regarded as an important issue. The selected contract of the lowest tender price might well result in a building that would be more expensive to maintain during its lifetime, with little thought given to the installation and functioning of services. Firms which tendered but failed to be selected would seek to recover the undisclosed costs of their bids by absorbing the expense in a successful contract with a subsequent client.

Many clients were already trying alternative approaches, ranging from two-stage tendering, where a contractor was selected before the design was much advanced, to the package deal where the contractor, often a manufacturer of standard buildings or systems, undertook the full service including design. This was the industry context in which JT sought to offer a rational building service. An article entitled *The Way We Work*, written in 1972 by Roger Mortimer, was published by JT Building Group for clients, architects and other professionals who, the company said, 'would like to know why we claim our approach to be particularly successful.'

The article claimed that the industry's existing arrangements were entirely arbitrary. 'They do not stem from any deliberate attempt to create the best framework for producing good buildings. The present divisions are the result of a conscious movement by nineteenth-century architects to develop a separate 'profession'. The motives then were misguided, but the idea of the gentleman architect, remote from the practical consequences of his art and the sordid world of actual building, is at the root of the twentieth century fragmentation of the industry.'

While building work was technically more complex during the twentieth century, JT argued that 'this makes close co-operation between the various skills even more essential. Only in building is there normally a significant separation between the design and production functions… this leaves a large area of potential conflict with each side devoting time and effort to laborious communication systems designed to protect their 'side' when inevitable disputes occur.'

JT, claiming it 'attracted staff who really enjoy seeing projects built and in use,' sought to persuade potential clients that its procedure reduced the industry's conventional risks. 'We have recognised that providing clients with the right building, on time and within budget, can most readily be achieved when architect, engineer, quantity surveyor, project manager and other essential skills work together as a team, removing traditional professional barriers.'

JT's methods

Design and build, JT believed, was proving more popular because clients recognised that it was an easier process. The client instructed one firm only and that firm took total responsibility for the project, including the co-ordination of professional services. A fixed-price fixed-period contract was offered. However, JT argued, clients needed to beware of firms offering package deals which might not be formulated in the right way. 'Some are not really a package at all, just an ad hoc assembly of builder/architect/engineer etc, each firm with its own interests to protect within the façade of a team. Others are so large that bureaucracy has taken over…We believe that the service will only be really effective when the different skills work together in a close-knit team.'

To promote its methods, JT emphasised:

Single-point responsibility, enabling the control of design and quality standards, tight control of costs and the reduction of overheads.

Value for money tenders on a fixed-price basis with JT operating on a cash flow basis, without outside finance, and so with the certainty of contract completion.

Ability to deal with major or minor changes in the contract and flexibility in negotiation and process.

Design solutions, well-informed within the company and, if and when necessary, quickly adapted during the construction.

Fast-tracking, with the project time shortened by overlapping design with construction.

Computer-aided design

It was early in the 1970s that JT launched a pioneering initiative: the adoption of computer-aided design for reinforced concrete structures, a technique at that time which was singularly lacking in the construction industry but which the company was to use extensively. In 1968, JT had consulted with IBM and, on its advice, John Pontin travelled to Marseilles to meet Yves Jallut of a French engineering consultancy which had a computer-based structural design system. Jallut's efficient programs led to JT managing two projects of reinforced concrete high-rise apartments in Paris.

The programs enabled the company, with IBM equipment, to set up Building Computer Services to make fast preparation of design and production drawings together with quantities and estimates. The conversion of (metric) French engineering programs for UK use was carried out by in-house software engineers, under the leadership of John

Crew. Computer-aided techniques, JT stated, could reduce staff requirements drastically for the design of structures. 'The benefits of the system include the ability to process design work very quickly, the saving of reinforcement due to more thorough calculation, and the accuracy, consistency and completeness of information, including quantities of concrete, shuttering and steel.' The system was marketed to other contracting companies and public authorities. Already, by the end of 1972, some 60 computer-aided projects had been designed, including flats, schools, offices, factories, shopping centres and multi-storey car parks.

Project teams

Design and build remained the core of JT's strategy. Roger Mortimer's article *The Way We Work* explained in detail the company's procedures and working practices for a typical project. 'In all cases the client provides a team to represent him. This may consist of a works manager, a property director or similar, who is a member of the client's staff. Very often he will be supported by outside professionals, architects, surveyors etc., working in a consultative capacity. The resultant group we refer to as the client team, and we serve the client through that team.'

JT formed a specific project team, co-ordinated by the directors. 'Once the client team is appointed, our project team works with it to establish the design brief,' the article stated. 'We regard brief building as an interactive process, whereby – in continuous contact – architect, constructor and client explore different solutions. The implications of a written brief are seldom apparent until sketch drawings are started, and the opportunities of a site become apparent. The benefit of our system at this stage is the completeness of the project team in terms of skills. Whatever the brief within our office, we can rapidly find its implications. Designs are developed with the certain knowledge that they can be constructed logically and will be within the agreed cost limits.' The company believed that its quality of design could match that of competing architectural practices.

After receiving the initial requirements from the client, and making the normal planning enquiries and preliminary site investigations, an outline scheme and price was presented to the client. Alterations and additions to existing buildings would almost certainly cause more complications than new structures. The presentation might vary from a single sketch drawing to a more detailed brochure, which the client might use to sell the idea to his colleagues or bankers. A project manager would be concerned with the overall planning and co-ordination. 'Within our office, the role of project manager is as critical at this stage as later,' the article stated. 'Often mainly behind the scenes, he is nevertheless making sure that the scheme is buildable within time and cost limits. When the scheme is put forward, he has helped to create it and he personally takes responsibility for living up to the promises made to the client and our own company.

'Working in the team will be the senior architects and technicians, the buyer, quantity surveyor, engineer and land surveyor. Because they all work in a group in an open office, there is less need for formal meetings of the team, though project meetings are periodically called to review progress or cope with major changes in plan. Generally, consultation consists of three or four people gathering around the most convenient desk – a great saving in time over conventional meetings.'

Once the initial proposals were accepted by the client, the work of detailed design would proceed, covering the usual statutory approvals and contract documentation. The article claimed: 'One difference between our service and the 'traditional' process of design, tender and build is that we are able to truncate the total design and build period considerably by overlapping detailed design and construction.'

In the construction stages, the responsibility for day-to-day supervision rested with JT's site agent. 'His role is critical in the maintenance of quality, timing and cost. He is visited regularly by project management and the project architect, and relies on the project buyer to keep him supplied with materials,' Roger's article stated. 'Office support to the site is of crucial importance, and it is particularly important to answer queries promptly to avoid site delay…Part of the service of the company is its post-contract aspect – we never wriggle when a post-completion defect occurs. Whether it is a design or workmanship defect, it is our problem as far as the client is concerned, and we put it right. Because of our integrated nature, the feedback of experience is immediate and we try to learn from every problem and build in the benefits on the next occasion.'

As John Pontin recalled later: 'If we didn't get it right – we paid to get it right.'

Individual responsibility

The Way We Work article emphasised that 'as with all organisations, it is the people who create success or failure. We can help them by providing an environment in which they see themselves making an effective contribution to a joint aim. This can be achieved by cutting out wasteful administrative work, by keeping the team to a size where everyone is close to the centre, and by giving maximum responsibility to individuals.'

Office staff, which totalled about 55 people in the early 1970s, each worked in a project team rather than a department. 'Day to day, they have practical responsibility to the management of that team, but also have technical responsibility to the senior man in the company in their particular field. For instance, an architect must meet the team's demands for information, but can rely on the senior architect to provide technical support over particular problems.

'As far as our architects are concerned, their role is of course very similar to that of their colleagues in other offices, in other words, they design buildings. In our case, however, they do not have to spend up to 30 per cent of their time on non-creative administrative work, as much of this is done by their colleagues in the team who are better placed to do it. For instance, when our architects need to know the availability of particular components, the project buyer is able to take the chore of telephone calls and correspondence with suppliers off his hands.' (JT had not employed women architects during that time) 'When things have to be changed, the architect does not have to write variation orders to the builder – his colleague at the next desk is the builder. The responsibility for detailed supervision of work on site belongs to project management, with the architect visiting mainly to keep in touch with the realities of the site and to help in the interpretation of his details.'

Thus, the article stated, the architect was able to concentrate on the work that he had been trained to do. 'Similarly, project management spends less time chasing for information, and no time in tedious wrangles over correct interpretation of instructions. The information is generated by the architects at adjoining desks who can consult him at the right time – the design stage. The project manager can thus concentrate on his key role of progress, quality and cost control. In this he is assisted by the team's quantity surveyor, who provides information on which the original estimate of cost is based. Again, because the bill of quantities is for internal use by the company, it can be prepared in a simple operational bill form, more suited to the practical requirements of the building process than standard method bills.

'Staff work together on a continuing basis and this creates a consistent approach to constructional details. While we have no formal 'system' of construction, certain solutions emerge as satisfactory answers to regular needs and the cost implications of these solutions are known. The role of the buyer is not just buying a component already precisely specified in a bill of quantities – he can make constructive suggestions at the design stage.'

A challenging environment

While some specialists – such as a land surveyor, planner and accountant – would work for all of the teams, the teams would be organised to be as self reliant as possible, with their own secretaries. 'There is no insistence on highly developed 'standard procedures' – group responsibility implies freedom to choose methods of work that draw the best from the individuals in the team,' the article continued. 'Only a skeleton of overall policy exists, mainly unwritten and adopted because it works – the movement of staff between teams also provides some consistency of methods.

'The picture then is of a very informal organisation in its internal communications, informal to the extent of apparent chaos at times. The scene in our open-plan offices, when everyone is there, has been likened to a newspaper office shortly before the paper goes to press. It is this feeling of involvement that creates commitment. There are no ivory towers in sight, but we think our buildings compare well with the admittedly questionable standard of the industry as a whole.'

JT regarded its office organisation as being dependent upon the physical environment. 'We have almost all our staff on a single office floor, and the elimination of the traditional 'departments' or professional pyramids has been achieved physically as well as organisationally. It is a challenging environment and not everyone is suited to it, but the great majority get satisfaction from practising their individual skill in a productive atmosphere. This job satisfaction must mean job satisfaction for the client.'

Meetings of senior staff would be held once or twice a month to discuss progress and policy in all fields, including financial. 'The effort is naturally concentrated on problem areas, but long-term aims are constantly reviewed. As with the rest of the company formality is minimal, and contentious matters will be talked out rather than voted upon, and many subjects that would be regarded as more suitable for the board room in most companies are discussed openly and decided by executive members and senior staff of the company.' Roger's article emphasised: 'It is only because we have capable staff at all levels, and provide a working environment in which they can perform unusually effectively, that we can live up to our claims in terms of service to the client.'

Flexibility as keynote

JT, claiming 'we are always interested to discuss new relationships in the world of building,' did offer variations of its design and build service. 'Although we are convinced that a totally integrated design and build service gives the best chance of providing the best value for money, we accept that there may be times when it cannot be adopted,' it stated. 'As flexibility is the keynote of our working methods, we are able to adapt to somewhat different relationships with a client and his project, and because of the completeness of our resources and the fact that we are used to working in a multi-professional situation, we can contribute considerable expertise.'

The company might agree to a negotiated contract service, when the architect and quantity surveyor were appointed by the client. It could also provide a consultant contractor service, working with an architect on a fee-basis, with the client having no commitment to use JT as contractors. If the client subsequently commissioned the company to build the project, the fee was absorbed into its overheads.

During the 1970s, the company faced competition from other construction companies, such as Shepherd and Kyle Stewart, which had adopted the design and build concept. To win contracts, the quality of the design, cost competitiveness and the project schedule were all essential and JT became skilled at competing against local and national rivals. 'Having often complained about being misunderstood because of rarity, JT now had more than ever to achieve satisfied clients,' Roger stated. 'JT's special ingredient often seemed to be the totally committed project team that presented itself at interviews and demonstrated total knowledge of the product they had developed and were offering.

'The project team's way of working was now completely natural to the company,' he added. 'The open atmosphere made it easy for all to input their expertise to the challenge of the project. Communications were greatly simplified and each project contributed to the collective knowledge of the team. The inevitable problems were not met with the departmental excuses so much seen in less integrated organisations.'

Schemes completed

Examples of the wide variety of JT's projects of the early years included:

DURDHAMSIDE FLATS, BRISTOL

Three blocks, totalling 82 flats, were built near Bristol's Durdham Downs in the early 1970s. The client was Hazelwood Flats Ltd, owned by David Perry, and with the flats to be sold on long leases. The site was surrounded by mature trees providing seclusion, but with the blocks in a staggered formation enabling them to have more sunlight and panoramic views. It was decided that the blocks should be varied in height to echo the skyline of the surrounding trees. To retain as much open space as possible, while allowing for plenty of parking, there were semi-basement car parks partially under the blocks. Where the garage podium was exposed, the roofs were paved, or planted and grassed, to provide a pleasant outlook from the overlooking flats. Such refinements had not been seen in Bristol. The site was fully landscaped and external facing bricks chosen because of their similarity to the colour of freestone used on nearby buildings. It was the first major development of private flats for sale in Bristol. Another five apartment developments, all on difficult and visually sensitive sites, were designed and built in the city.

HOTEL IN BRISTOL

In 1970, Esso Motor Hotels asked for a design and build package of 156 bedrooms, conference rooms and restaurant on a site surrounded by orchards and fields. 'The building was designed around this landscape and only one mature tree was felled together with a few orchard trees,' JT recorded. Although the contract was scheduled to be completed by May 31 1972, the kitchen was handed over to the client for equipping in March and public areas and bedrooms were partially handed over for furnishing in April. This enabled Esso Motor Hotels to start letting bedrooms on June 1. JT said: 'This is one example of the capabilities in design, organisation, speed of construction and co-operation which the JT Building Group offers to clients.'

TEMPLE WAY HOUSE, BRISTOL

The office building with parking for 140 cars was completed in 1975 as the head offices of Clerical, Medical & General Assurance, one of the first large insurance companies to move its headquarters from London. The 140,000 sq ft of offices with five passenger lifts were on a busy inner circuit road which influenced the design of its façade, with large precast concrete panels and narrow, gold-coloured reflective double-glazed windows. It was one of the first fully air-conditioned and 'deep plan' office buildings in Bristol and a remarkably large project to be entrusted to a young company.

EUROTHERM, WORTHING

Eurotherm, based in Worthing and later to be a subsidiary of Invensys, is one of the leading electronic suppliers of control and measurement instrumentation. When it was a private company, it negotiated a site on the outskirts of Worthing for a new headquarters. It decided with Gleeds, building consultants, to use design and build and invited four firms to submit tenders. JT, however, was the only one which used in-house design. The others were builders who employed private architects on an ad hoc basis.

JT's tender was not the lowest cost 'but they liked our design, and approach and general attitude,' Roger Mortimer noted. 'Their project manager said afterwards that the three other architects spent too much time on outside appearance, without understanding the practical needs of the brief. At the formal presentation to the board, we put great emphasis on the integrated JT design and build approach.' Almost immediately after JT was appointed, Eurotherm's successful public flotation caused a rethink. The management preferred a single-storey 4,700 sq m. building with a more

Durdhamside flats. Photo: Stephen Morris

Temple Way House. Photo: Stephen Morris

modern approach, with little differentiation to be made between its offices and production space. So JT redesigned and re-quoted. The design, with a precast concrete column and low-profile steel roof structure, had a large open-plan main building. A simple structure was made distinctive with a streamlined image and good detailing and materials. Continuous glazing was protected by brise soleil where it was needed. 'It was a far cry from many industrial facilities of the time,' according to Roger. He recalled that JT had an energetic site agent and the project manager, architect, engineers and buyers attended all the meetings with the client and advisers. On occasions, they would go out together for a social evening, reflecting the friendly and co-operative sense of mission. The building was completed on time with a 2.1 per cent increase in the contract cost which was entirely due to the client's extra requirements. 'The project was profitable to JT and proved a very useful reference for future work,' Roger commented.

HIGH KINGSDOWN, BRISTOL

A private housing development, it was built between 1970 and 1974 at a cost of £1.5m. Whicheloe Macfarlane Partnership was commissioned by Bristol City Council to prepare the overall scheme on a seven-acre site, derelict after wartime bombing and close to Bristol University. It was then offered by tender to developers. JT made a successful bid for the site and its architects then prepared the detailed scheme. The development was of 103 yellow-brick and red-tiled courtyard houses and 110 six-storey flats, including 40 units for elderly people, and a supermarket. It was arranged in tight L-shaped zig-zag terraces between a system of footways, with high walls to give privacy and sheltered courtyard gardens. Garages were on the perimeter and no through traffic was allowed. A 'village square' was formed around a retained Victorian pub.

'The project has revitalised this part of the city, and provided a new housing area with a distinctive architectural character,' JT declared. 'The actual building process had many problems, often arising from the extensive old foundations which had to be cleared. The need to keep pace with sales by building in phases was another complication, as was the draining and servicing of the interlocking courtyard housing.' The scheme won four national awards and is still visited as a pioneer of dense but low-rise inner city development.

CLIFTON COLLEGE POOL AND SPORTS HALL, BRISTOL

JT described this as being a 'complicated combination of new building and conversion of existing spaces in a very restricted site.' The work in 1981 had to be programmed around the school holidays, with staged handovers of different sections of the work. The whole structural frame was craned in over the buildings surrounding the site. The work was completed in 10 months, four months ahead of schedule. Similar projects were carried out for Radley College in Oxfordshire and Harrow School.

High Kingsdown,
1970-74:
high-density,
low-rise.

SOUTH CAMBRIDGESHIRE DISTRICT COUNCIL OFFICES

A contract for the council's new headquarters was advertised in 1983 and 65 firms applied. The £1.6m winning tender from JT was £82,000 cheaper than its nearest rival and nearly £400,000 less than the highest tender. The inclusive price for the structural concrete was nearly £200,000 less than the average of the other bids. The savings were largely due to lower quantities than expected as a result of JT's in-house computer techniques.

Roger Mortimer told *Architectural Journal* in August 1984: 'The computer work is coupled with a critical review of buildability. Our programs have consistently given very economical results for the frame element of office buildings. We use them for all the detailing and scheduling because they can do masses of analysis very quickly, and give our engineers the power to look at alternatives more completely.' *Architectural Journal* quoted the client's quantity surveyors, who stated: 'Traditionally we always slaughter the poor architect's work when we need to cut costs, but here the saving was in the structure.'

6 The Arnolfini partnership
Shared route to Bush House

A simple corner of the real world had suddenly been fixed on to a panel as by magic…It is as if we could pay a visit to the Arnolfini in their house.
E.H.Gombrich: Van Eyck's portrait of the Arnolfini couple
(*The Story of Art*, Phaidon 1966)

In the same year when JT was founded, in 1961, so too in Bristol was Arnolfini which became, and is, one of the country's leading centres for the visual and performing arts. With free admission to its building and open seven days a week, it attracts up to half a million visitors a year. Its declared purpose, ever since its beginning, is 'to seek out challenging, often controversial and sometimes relatively unknown artists and performers and to provide a vital showcase for their work.'

Since the 1960s, a remarkable bond has been maintained between JT and Arnolfini, with its association between business and the arts enhancing cultural life in the city and region. From the mid-1970s, Arnolfini has been at Bush House on Narrow Quay, when the nineteenth-century warehouse (named after its previous owners) was converted by JT. Today, Arnolfini owns the entire six-storey building, with a big redevelopment completed in summer 2005 with expanded and upgraded galleries and spaces. But it was first started by just three people above a bookshop in the Clifton district of Bristol: Jeremy Rees, described then as a printing manager, John Orsborn, a Bristol-based artist, and Annabel Lawson. Annabel (who married Jeremy in 1962) had studied textile design at Chelsea School of Art and the Central School of Art in London.

Jeremy, who was to become Arnolfini's director for 25 years, was born in 1937 in Bridgwater, Somerset. His father Glyn, a fiery Welshman, was a skilled craftsman who taught woodwork and metalwork at the local grammar school, and was a keen amateur violin player who took charge of the school orchestra. His mother Jean, an artist, was a founder member of Bridgwater Arts Centre, of which she became chair and later president. Glyn was also involved with the film programme at the arts centre from its inception in 1946. Jeremy went to Taunton School where he became, he said, 'enthused with art – I had a new art master who was very good.' Interested in fine printing, he took up a traineeship with the Bristol printing and packaging firm of Allen Davies and a three-year course at the London College of Printing. While in London he made frequent visits to the Institute of Contemporary Arts (ICA), which had been co-founded in 1947 by Herbert Read, the influential art critic and friend of Picasso, and Roland Penrose, the surrealist painter and poet. Both men still presided over the ICA during the period when Jeremy visited. He recalled, 'I thought at the time there was nothing like this in Bristol and I'd try to start up something.'

After National Service, he rejoined Allen Davies and then went to work with a typographic designer, Ron Ford. JT commissioned logos and stationery from Ron Ford, resulting in Jeremy's first contact with the company. Jeremy, determined to launch a contemporary arts enterprise in Bristol, discussed his idea with the recently-formed South West Arts, the first regional organisation of its kind in the country. But he could obtain no funding. 'Who was likely to put up capital for such a venture, promoted by someone with no track record in the field?' he remarked. Meanwhile, he was offered a post at the Bath Academy of Art at Corsham. He decided to work there only part-time, as a lecturer of typographic design, to enable him to set up a Bristol gallery 'without wasting any more time.'

The academy had been founded as early as 1852, when it was called the Bath School of Art and Design to encourage training in design to support manufacture. After bomb damage during the Second World War, it was re-established in 1946 as the Bath Academy of Art at Corsham, several miles east of Bath. Its principal was Clifford Ellis, who inspired Jeremy and others who taught there, with the academy gaining a high reputation. 'Corsham was a very interesting place at that time – Clifford Ellis was a quite exceptional person,' Jeremy remembered. Among the tutors and visiting artists at the academy – and whose works were to be later shown at Arnolfini – were Kenneth Armitage, Gillian Ayres, Henry Cliffe, Michael Craig-Martin, Howard Hodgkin, Richard Hamilton, and Peter Lanyon and Terry Frost, both associated with the St Ives School of artists. (The academy was closed at Corsham and subsumed into Bath College of Higher Education in 1983. It was renamed Bath School of Art and Design and then brought into Bath Spa University College)

Naming the gallery

To open Arnolfini, Jeremy and his two partners, John Orsborn and Annabel Lawson, each put up £100 and leased a 1,200 sq ft (111 sq m) space, which had been a joinery workshop above the Triangle West bookshop in Clifton. The converted, whitewashed loft was a short walk away from Bristol University, the City Museum & Art Gallery and the Royal West of England Academy, founded in 1844 as the city's first art gallery. The RWA, in an imposing Victorian building, was 'very, very conservative,' Jeremy recalled, no doubt, at the time, hoping that their own gallery would be seen as an impudently lively rival. He remembered 'When we opened Arnolfini, I wanted an inscription above the door – Enjoy yourself!'

Annabel and Jeremy Rees with John Orsborn at Arnolfini's first show on Triangle West, March 1961. The painting is Peter Swan's *Child with Tricycle*.

The partners named the gallery after the masterpiece by the Flemish painter Jan Van Eyck of the merchant Giovanni Arnolfini and his wife. The work, painted in 1434 and probably intended as a celebration of their betrothal, is in the National Gallery, London. 'Finding a suitable name for the planned new gallery proved difficult and finally Arnolfini was chosen – as a name that people would remember, even if they misspelt it,' Jeremy said. Van Eyck's painting could be loosely interpreted as relevant to Bristol and contemporary art: the merchant as a reminder of the city's seafaring trade, while the oil painting itself had been radical, with a richness and luminosity of colour, light and space. It depicted an intriguing portrait of the couple in a room where the artist was himself portrayed in a convex wall mirror. (However, a future Arnolfini newsletter read: 'There is no deep symbolism connected with this choice which was simply a personal admiration for the painting')

With Jeremy as director, the partners opened the gallery in March 1961. The first exhibition was of drawings of harvesters by Josef Herman and paintings by Peter Swan, a Bristol artist who lectured at the West of England College of Art. It was reviewed by Derek Balmer, the photographer and artist who wrote a weekly arts column in the *Western Daily Press*. He was to hold several future shows at Arnolfini and, in 2001, became president of the revitalised Royal West of England Academy. Contemporary bronzes and exhibitions of paintings and prints followed as well as regular shows of contemporary jewellery. The jewellery was shown as one of the few such displays around the country and which, together with art works, were offered for sale. Open painting competitions were organised in 1962 and reviews began to appear in national newspapers. 'The sights have been kept high ever since, with exhibitions of both nationally known and local artists,' wrote the art critic Nevile Wallis. He described it as 'an illuminating experience, which many Bristolians ought to share.' But it was, he wrote, a 'precarious enterprise' discouraged by the 'segregated cultural life of Bristol'.

In November 1962, the partners sponsored the formation of the New Bristol Arts Club to encourage other art-related events, including drama, films, jazz performances and poetry readings – on one occasion, by the American beat poet Alan Ginsberg. 'We said visual art doesn't exist in a vacuum,' Jeremy said. 'We were interested in putting them into a wider context and this was very much influenced by my going to the ICA.' (The club's activities, though, were to cease, mainly because of the lack of suitable premises)

Trustees chosen

For the first two years, Annabel and Orsborn's wife Jenny staffed the gallery unpaid and the budget did not run to the installation of a telephone. The first secretary/assistant was employed in 1963, when Orsborn left and Gwen Lawson became a partner. Jeremy, whose sister Caroline worked at Arnolfini during that time, was still the unpaid director and, requiring the income, became a full-time teacher at Bath Academy in 1965. With the need to organise the gallery's finances – and to find the money to insulate its chilly roof – the partners decided that year to set up a non-profitmaking company with charitable status, Arnolfini Gallery Ltd. The Arts Council gave a guarantee against loss and made a revenue grant of £1,100 while the city council contributed a modest grant of £350.

A council of management was formed with Peter and Caroline Barker-Mill chosen as trustees and directors. The Barker-Mill family had been landowners in Hampshire for centuries and, after the Second World War, much of their land was acquired for Southampton's expansion. Peter, born in 1908 and himself an artist, gifted 750 acres to form the Roydon Woods Nature Reserve at Lymington. He and his wife Caroline lived at Wookey Hole in Somerset and became frequent visitors to Arnolfini, enjoying the exhibitions. 'Peter reluctantly agreed to become chairman and subsequently became an incredibly generous benefactor,' Jeremy noted.

By 1966, the finances stabilised, enabling Jeremy to cease being a full-time teacher at Bath Academy and instead part-time again. In the year to April 1967, Arnolfini's income totalled about £5,500, although there was a net deficit of £2,250. During 1968, Peter established the Barker-Mill Trust as a substantial endowment fund for Arnolfini (valued at £230,000 in March 2000) and which included income from the family's tenanted farms. He also became patron of the Arnolfini Collection Trust. The trustees, with Peter's financial support, decided that year that it was imperative to have a full-time director to manage the expanding programme. Jeremy therefore took up the post, with the secretary/assistant as the other paid staff member. He encouraged business sponsorship, gallery sales of prints and paintings, picture loan schemes and educational and outreach activities.

During the same year a pioneering exhibition of new British sculpture was staged indoors and outdoors. It was opened by the Labour minister Jennie Lee, the first arts minister to be appointed and who passionately supported the arts. Collaborative exhibitions were held with the ICA and other organisations, and Arnolfini arranged shows around the West Country, especially at Dartington Hall in Devon. During the 1960s, there were exhibitions by Prunella Clough, John Furnival, David Inshaw, Ceri Richards and Bridget Riley, as well as by those who taught at Bath Academy.

A bigger home

At the start of the 1970s, the trustees agreed it was essential to find a larger home than the gallery at Triangle West. 'The present rented premises provide a good main exhibition area but there is very little storage space and no additional display space,' they reported. John Pontin had become a trustee of Arnolfini and JT also needed to move. The construction industry was booming and the company, which had a headquarters staff of about 100 people at Queen Charlotte Street, needed bigger premises. 'Our turnover within the building group was running at about 50 per cent compound growth since our existence and the disruption and cost of so many moves was well understood by us at this time,' John wrote later. 'Our last office in the central area of Bristol contained approx. 7,500 sq ft of space for our use and we were bulging at the seams.'

With Arnolfini searching for more space, JT offered it a warehouse which the company had acquired at 45 Queen Square, but only as a temporary home because the site was scheduled to be redeveloped. The handsome, tree-lined Georgian square, close to the Floating Harbour, was described by the architectural writer Nikolaus Pevsner as 'Bristol's major piece of early eighteenth-century town planning.' It had been the scene of violent riots and fires in 1831 sparked by the Reform Bill and, in 1936, the square was devastated again by the brutal construction of a dual carriageway road. As Pevsner commented, 'the worst the Bristol authorities have done is to cut this new traffic route diagonally across Queen Square.'

'Roger Mortimer drew up plans for a minimal conversion in Queen Square and we moved in 1970 and started our contemporary music programme,' Jeremy said. 'We were there for two and a half years.' Arnolfini, with twice the space it had occupied before, opened a bookshop and exhibitions included works by Frost, Hodgkin and Lanyon. In 1972, Jeremy helped organise a project to site sculpture in eight city centres.

Searching for a place

Arnolfini, soon having to depart from its temporary home, approached the city council to lease the Granary, a Bristol Byzantine brick building on the Welsh Back quayside and which was on the market. But this was acquired by another bidder. 'We started looking further afield,' Jeremy said. Bush Warehouse, as it was named by its previous owners, was seen as a possibility because it was empty and had one of the best waterfront locations in the city. The big, square-shaped stone building overlooked the Floating Harbour.

'The last male line of the Bush family had died and his widow put the building on the market through Midland Bank trustees,' Jeremy said. 'It went to auction and then the sale fell through – one of the reasons being that there was to be a new inner-circuit road which was to go through two bays of the building, plus the two Georgian houses next door. I wrote to the Midland Bank trustees to ask if we could make an offer. They didn't want to talk to us. But we persevered and they agreed they would sell it to us for, I think, £65,000. It was still under risk that we might lose two bays. But at that time the city was talking about a new museum and art gallery – its museum had been damaged during the war. The councillors decided to have the new building on Castle Green [close to the city's main shopping centre] and brought in Hugh Casson as consultant.'

Arnolfini's trustees contemplated having a purpose-built development adjacent to the scheme. 'We reached a point where we decided whether to take an option on Bush Warehouse or to do the development on Castle Green. The council of management took a vote and decided, on balance,

Jeremy Rees (left) with the Arnolfini team at 45 Queen Square, April 1971.

that we should go for Castle Green. So we lost interest in Bush Warehouse at that point.' The trustees commissioned Casson as the architect, with JT as the potential developers.

'Then there was a change in policy in relation to the funding of capital projects by local authorities,' Jeremy said. 'And Bristol had to decide between an incinerator at Avonmouth or a new city museum and art gallery.' The council chose the incinerator. 'Casson said, 'Never mind, there's a piece of land by Bristol Bridge and I think we can do a scheme there.' So he got consent from the city to work with us on this alternative scheme, which wasn't an ideal site, very narrow, but it was just about possible.' The scheme was a complex of galleries, a waterside restaurant and a 450-seat cinema and performance space. Application for planning consent was made in 1971. According to *Bristol Evening Post*, 'the city authorities dithered, dithered again and finally threw out the planning application.' Jeremy recalled: 'What happened was that Casson also had to put in his proposals for the landscaping of Castle Green. The council accepted his proposals for that and turned down Arnolfini. We were back to Square One. So we moved our attention back to Bush Warehouse – we were still working with JT on all these schemes.'

The local authority's plan to demolish part of the warehouse, in order to build a four-lane road bridge across St. Augustine's Reach, was still a threat but never implemented. A property developer, however, was seeking to demolish the whole building to erect an office block. After protracted negotiations, and when property prices were rising sharply, JT acquired a 999-year leasehold and renamed it Bush House to be its headquarters and the home of Arnolfini. It was to be the pioneering mixed-use building after the Floating Harbour had become almost moribund.

Port's History

Bush Warehouse, in the days when the port had been thriving, was built in Victorian times on a quayside corner of the Floating Harbour and St Augustine's Reach, which had been channelled as early as the thirteenth century to divert the river Frome to join the river Avon. The opposite and west side of the reach was named Canon's Marsh, originally a salt marsh used by the canons of St Augustine's Abbey for grazing and orchards. The abbey was converted to Bristol Cathedral after the dissolution of the monasteries.

Since the Middle Ages, Bristol had prospered with the export of woollen cloth manufactured in the region and it became one of the busiest ports in England, despite being seven miles inland. In 1497 John Cabot set out from Bristol and crossed the Atlantic to discover the 'New Founde Landes'. (Cabot Tower, on Brandon Hill overlooking the city, was erected to mark the 400th anniversary of his voyage. In 1985, his bronze statue by Stephen Joyce was placed on the quayside outside Bush House) The Society of Merchant Venturers – of which John Pontin is a member and which today funds charitable activities including education and sheltered accommodation – was established in 1552 to control and promote trade in the city. Until 1807, when the British slave trade was abolished, about 2,100 ships sailed from Bristol to transport from Africa an estimated half a million of black people across the Atlantic to America. Bristol was also importing and exporting a broad range of commodities. Its population in the 1770s was estimated at 35,400.

Visually, Bristol has always been an exceptional city because of the quayside waterways in its centre, which led Alexander Pope, the eighteenth century satirist and poet, to exclaim: 'In the middle of the street, as far as you can see, hundreds of ships, their masts as thick as they can stand by one another, which is the oddest and most surprising sight imaginable.' Robert Louis Stevenson's *Treasure Island*, published in 1883 but set in the eighteenth century, quoted Jim Hawkins when meeting Long John Silver in Bristol: 'On our little walk along the quays, he made himself the most interesting companion, telling me about the different ships that passed by, their rig, tonnage, and nationality, explaining their work – how one was discharging, another taking in cargo, and a third making ready for sea.'

The phrase 'all shipshape and Bristol fashion' is believed to have originated in the eighteenth century, when boats needed to be stoutly built because the twisting river Avon could cause them to be stranded on mud at low tide. In 1803, the river was dammed to form the Floating Harbour with ships able to berth at a constant high-water level. Silt and sewage, however, accumulated in the harbour and so Brunel in 1832 designed a dredger and sluices, known as the Underfall. Until 1848, the docks were in private ownership and were then taken over by the city council.

Canon's Marsh became an industrial area of manufacture, transit sheds, railway sidings, timber yards and tobacco warehouses. But ever-bigger ships were unable to enter the narrow harbour locks. The port steadily lost trade to the Avonmouth deepwater docks, constructed in 1877, and to docks built two years later at Portishead. The Floating Harbour remained active for many more decades (a tower was erected temporarily on Bush House's roof with a mechanical elevator to distribute grain to bin-silos). However, the decline of trade was inevitable not only because of ship sizes but because other ports, on the east and south coasts, were gaining trade with the continent rather than North America.

Waterfront's revival

During the mid twentieth century, the city authorities covered over part of St Augustine's Reach in order to build a road traffic circuit. In 1970, the Bristol Corporation Act was passed to end navigation rights and, while this was not in fact implemented it confirmed the port's commercial demise. The last shipyard, Albion Yard owned by Charles Hill & Sons, was finally closed in 1977. Canon's Marsh itself, of some 66 acres, became semi-derelict with the port's transit sheds and warehouses made redundant, while the city council failed to encourage renovation for new uses. It even considered filling in parts of the harbour to allow office development.

Bush House, when bought by JT on a 999-year lease, had been rapidly deteriorating and, as Jeremy Rees remembered, it was 'full of pigeons'. The warehouse needed complete restoration, at much expense, and would take considerable work and time before JT and Arnolfini would be ready to move into it. JT had to gain planning consent for what is a Grade II listed building, classified as a particularly important building of more than special architectural or historic interest. Consent would have been unlikely if the building was used only for offices but the authorities accepted 'planning gain' in which JT promoted a mixed-use development with the arts centre benefiting the local community.

JT itself was a contradiction among property developers. 'The use by a design and build organisation of the upper floors of a converted warehouse for their new offices may seem somewhat perverse when new office blocks predominate,' the company stated. 'But the situation is exceptional: a fine position, central but not congested (with moorings outside), a plan shape suited to the needs of a flexible organisation, and a building full of character…One great benefit of the occupation of this building by Arnolfini is the life and interest that such a use will generate in the area. With the disappearance of dockside activity the danger of a somewhat deserted atmosphere is obvious.'

Patrick Brown, then chairman of Bristol Civic Society, wrote to the *Bristol Evening Post*: 'We are encouraged, not only because this means a prolonged life for an old building, but because this is a landmark of considerable architectural merit, and because it promises to bring people – Bristolians – back into the area, to enjoy the waterfront… May we hope that this will give heart to others with ideas and imagination?'

7 Bush House as a home
Reviving the derelict docklands

Whatever you can do, or dream you can, begin it. Boldness has genius, power and magic in it. Johann Wolfgang von Goethe (1749-1832)

Bush House was to prove the first revival of Bristol's desolate docklands, and one of the first examples of how the arts could stimulate economic as well as social regeneration in UK cities.

The nation's economy was in trouble from autumn 1973, when Arab oil-producing states quadrupled the price of oil. Miners and power workers, demanding wage rises, imposed an overtime ban which resulted in power cuts, causing the prime minister Edward Heath to declare a state of emergency in the winter and impose a three-day working week. In February 1974, the Conservative Government was defeated by Labour. Although John Pontin was well aware, during the political and economic upheaval, that the warehouse project was a calculated risk, he considered it to be a 'marvellous opportunity to bring a new dimension to the centre of Bristol. Hopefully, it will inspire others to bring new life to similar buildings.'

Reconstruction of Bush House took 18 months and, meanwhile, Arnolfini's temporary tenure at Queen Square was ending. Jeremy Rees said: 'Bush House had to be gutted and we set our eyes on W-shed, which was owned by the city council.' JT had acquired short-term leases for the disused shed and the adjacent E-shed. The transit sheds, built in the late nineteenth century on the west side of St. Augustine's Reach, had been used for the cargo brought in and out of the Floating Harbour, with a railway linked to the original Temple Meads station designed by Brunel. (The first train between London and Bristol ran in 1841.) By the end of the 1960s, these sheds had fallen into disuse.

Arnolfini moved into the W-shed in 1973 although the city council showed 'considerable reluctance', according to Jeremy. 'The council were extremely suspicious that we were trying to get our foot in the door there and would never get us out again.' JT made a minimal conversion of the W-shed for Arnolfini, giving it a larger gallery than it had occupied at Queen Square, together with a small arts cinema, a bookshop with space to exhibit jewellery, and a café-bar overlooking the harbour. By subsidising the arts venue on one floor, with commercial and retail uses on the ground floor, it was to be a pioneering example of the mutually beneficial mix of art and commerce. Paul Overy, art critic for *The Times*, wrote in June 1973: 'Unfortunately this building is to be pulled down in two years'

time as part of the wholesale destruction of its old city centre which Bristol, like other provincial cities, seems hell-bent on in the commercial struggle to put up as many prestige offices and expense-account hotels as possible. This ought to be vigorously resisted.'

In due course, the sheds were saved. In the 1970s, Bristol Exhibition Centre was run by Ray Purnell in two other sheds, U and V-sheds. Events there included the World Wine Fair, which attracted up to 80,000 visitors a year, a beer festival and classic car show. The head leases of U and V-sheds were acquired by JT, giving it unified ownership of the stretch of sheds along the west side of St Augustine's Reach. Arnolfini also staged musical events at the W-shed, with Richard Hawkins programming the music, then succeeded by Judith Serota (who later became executive director of the Spitalfields Festival.) Clive Adams was recruited for the new post of exhibitions co-ordinator in 1974. The shows included photography and the first Arts Council touring exhibition at Arnolfini, 'Beyond Painting and Sculpture', curated by Richard Cork. Works by Bridget Riley were staged jointly with the City Art Gallery. The cinema, with British Film Institute support, was programmed by David Hopkins, who was responsible for the first festival of independent cinema at W-shed in February 1975. By then, there were about 80,000 annual visitors.

Building work

As the reconstruction of Bush House got underway, JT knew it to be much more difficult and time-consuming than a new-build project. The design and build work was led by the architects Roger Mortimer and Mike Duckering and the structural engineer Bob Evans, of JT's Building Computer Services. Project management was by Howard Williams and Peter Bray and site management by Ron Lane and Mike Peel. The original design of the warehouse was attributed to Richard Shackleton Pope and built in the 1830s. It was owned by Acramans, described as 'iron and tin plate merchants, iron and brass founders & ironmongers, manufacturers of patent proved chain cables and anchors.'

The warehouse had impressive proportions, with a combination of Regency neo-classicism and the chunkiness of later 'Bristol Byzantine' warehouses. Dark-grey pennant stone contrasted with Bath stone dressings and its rectangular windows were recessed within tall round arches. Pevsner described it as 'a big Bristolian warehouse in the Rundbogenstil built remarkably early.' (Rundbogenstil was an architectural style, based on the round arch, which had been introduced in Germany) Although the building was described as a tea warehouse, tea was never the only commodity stored there as it was used for Acramans' various trades in the port. Acramans reputedly went bankrupt and, after intervening changes of ownership, their warehouse was taken over in 1846 by George and James Bush.

With its conversion, the external structure was retained almost intact but with new window frames and glazed entrances and the cleansing of the grubby pennant stone facades. The interior was gutted and rebuilt with an in-situ reinforced concrete structure of columns and 'waffle' floor slabs, all supported on new concrete piled foundations taken through the river silt. The massive stone walls remained supported on the original timber pile foundations. An extra storey was built under a metal-clad pyramidal roof with glazed mansard sides and services housed in the apex. Air-conditioned offices were on the upper four floors with a passenger lift from the entrance on Prince Street.

Arnolfini, on the ground and first floors with 18,000 sq ft (1,672 sq. m) of space, had an entrance and reception area on Narrow Quay, on the east side of St Augustine's Reach. It had a single large gallery on the ground floor, smaller galleries on the first floor and an auditorium which occupied both floor levels. The auditorium was designed to be flexible for cinema as well as live music, dance and multi-media events. It was equipped with quadraphonic sound, a lighting system and adaptable seating for up to 300 people. There was a library (which became a bookshop), dressing rooms, a workshop and administrative offices. Upstairs, there was a small coffee bar and downstairs a restaurant/bar, with a doorway onto the quayside. Trees were planted next to outdoor tables for people to sit and have drinks.

The scheme cost over £1m, of which Arnolfini's share was £431,000. Its development was made possible by £250,000 of private funds, with money donated by Peter Barker-Mill, and the main grants of £80,000 from the Arts Council, £20,000 from the Gulbenkian Foundation and £31,000 from the British Film Institute. Arnolfini paid JT a peppercorn rent of 5p a year on a 99-year lease but shared the building's service charges.

After the 1975 conversion had been completed, JT described the building's robust character as 'one of the most challenging projects carried out by JT. The complex planning involved in providing the elaborately serviced public facilities of Arnolfini within the shell of a listed building, and providing normal office space above, called for great ingenuity. The speed of construction within restrictions of existing walls, and the need to achieve a high quality of finish for direct decorations, especially in the gallery, needed careful site management. The basic decision by Arnolfini and JT was a considerable act of faith, now justified by the success of the completed project.'

The opening

Arnolfini's new home fulfilled the determination of Jeremy Rees to create the new environment of a nationally recognised regional centre for new and experimental arts. It was opened to the public in October 1975 by Lord Esher, chairman of the arts panel of the Arts Council, while its director of art, Robin Campbell, called Arnolfini 'an outstanding achievement in the field of the contemporary arts, and a shining example of imaginative vision allied to practical planning.' The opening exhibition was of paintings by Howard Hodgkin and, in the upper gallery, works by Keith Milow, a sculptor and printmaker. The Grimethorpe Colliery Band held a concert at the Victoria Rooms in Clifton to mark the occasion. The first film to be shown was *The Mother and the Whore* directed by Jean Eustache and there were lectures on jazz.

The opening attracted much national attention. John McEwen, *The Spectator* magazine's art critic, wrote that Arnolfini was 'more lavish and complete in its facilities as a modern art complex than any similar establishment anywhere else in the country, including London…Jeremy Rees deserved every hand-clap of the ovation he received at the opening.' An article by Bryan Little in *Country Life* stated: 'Bristol and the whole of the West of England have been given what the Arts Council representatives have declared to be a highly significant cultural institution, providing the best facilities of their kind in any English provincial centre.' William Feaver, art critic of *The Observer*, wrote 'the new

Jeremy and team: early days at Bush House.

Arnolfini gallery is well placed, midway between spiritual uplift and recreational pursuit…Certainly the grandest arts centre in the country, and probably the best appointed, it now has to prove itself as a bridgehead, helping artists and serving the public.'

An innovation at Bush House, to become a permanent part of Arnolfini's programmes, was contemporary dance. 'I was very interested in contemporary dance and when we moved into Narrow Quay we would have a dance programme,' Jeremy said. 'It would be suitable within the limitations of space for dance and performance as well as cinema.' The Welsh Dance Theatre put on opening performances and there followed collaboration with Ballet Rambert and what was to become Dance Umbrella, the annual contemporary dance festival which started in 1978. There was to be a growing involvement with schools, with children attending dance workshops and performances.

'JT helped to sponsor a number of our dance events,' Jeremy recalled. 'There were other major sponsors. Imperial Tobacco [headquartered in Bristol] ran a series of celebrity events, both concerts and dance. Our attitude was that people made such a mess of our floors with cigarettes – people in those days smoked everywhere – and as we had to clear up the mess we might as well take some money from Imperial. Harveys [the Bristol wine merchants] sponsored a lot of our music concerts, and IBM sponsored the opening at Bush House. And London Life [then based in Bristol] sponsored us during their short life.'

New offices

JT's own offices in Bush House were completed in April 1976 and proved a definite asset for the company's internal organisation as well as its revitalisation of the city's waterfront. 'It is particularly satisfying to have this fine nineteenth century building on the waterfront, and we now have all group activities co-ordinated from a single building,' John Pontin stated. All the design and build staff were on the open-plan and well-lit top floor. 'At the height of activity, it resembles more a newspaper office about to produce a first edition than a traditional builder's office,' John wrote. 'The atmosphere can be very stimulating which is one reason for our success, I believe.'

Roger Mortimer agreed that the building was especially appropriate for the 'dynamic operational style' of the company. 'Going ahead with the project, in a then-unglamorous part of the city centre and in a period of chaos and depression in the economy, was a brave act,' he commented. 'In part, it reflected John's feelings for Bristol's inner city and the

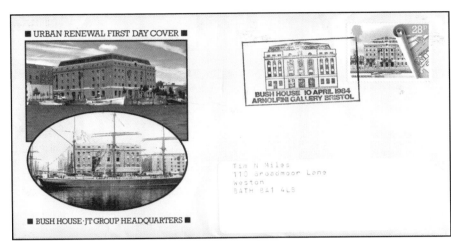

harbourside in particular. The long-standing interest in, and support for, the work of Arnolfini Gallery was another factor. Bush House also provided a chance to prove design and build's growing ability to handle important conservation work. It was much quoted as an example of imaginative recycling of redundant buildings.'

Bush House was later to be featured by Royal Mail on 28p stamps with the caption Urban Renewal – Bristol. The stamps, issued in 1984, marked the 150th anniversary of the Royal Institute of British Architects and the Chartered Institute of Building. To commemorate the issue, JT stated: 'Although the decision to restore Bush House was a calculated risk taken during the oil crisis of 1974, the results of this action have created a fine asset for the JT Group and the city of Bristol. The disused harbour has entered a new era and property values have been enhanced…The docks are a focal point of activity in central Bristol, putting the city firmly on the national and international tourist map.'

In the short term, other office space in Bush House was let to tenants, including Spandex, the supplier of materials to the sign and display industries, and firms providing services to JT, such as Progressive Structures. JT also set up Avon Business Centre (subsequently managed by Jackie Luxton) and providing fully-serviced small office suites and meeting rooms and which, it claimed, was the first such centre outside London. In his chairman's report, John remarked: 'Where else in Bristol would you find an office suite with a panorama of the centre of the city, taking in such fine views of St. Mary Redcliffe Church and the nearby Georgian terraces to the east and the slopes of Clifton and the Bristol Cathedral to the north-west – as well as the occasional view of waterborne vessels?'

With Arnolfini flourishing, many more people were coming to enjoy the character and atmosphere of the Floating Harbour. Powerboat races were held annually from the mid-1970s (although serious accidents and insufficient sponsorship caused the events to be abandoned at the end of the 1980s.) Bristol Industrial Museum was opened in 1978 by the city council in disused transit sheds on the south side of the Floating Harbour. The

Arnolfini interior, 1975.

museum displayed the city's history of aircraft and vehicle manufacture, shipping and printing. Outside the museum, four electric cranes remain on the quayside – previously there had been over 40 – and a steam train on the harbour railway and veteran harbour boats recall the days of the commercial port.

First two decades

In 1979, when JT acquired the freehold of Bush House for a nominal sum (its lease having been for 999 years), Peter Barker-Mill gave Arnolfini even more financial support by setting up the Ashley Clinton Endowment Fund (it was valued in March 2000 at £2.82m) During that decade, exhibitions at Arnolfini by artists, often at an early stage in their career, included works by Marcel Broodthaers, Patrick Caulfield, Richard Long, David Nash, Ed Ruscha and Allen Jones. Contemporary jewellery displayed at Arnolfini could prove remarkably novel - as reported in Designing Britain: a high new jewelleryism 1977-1985 (University of Brighton): 'An idiosyncratic jeweller Tom Saddington had himself welded into a 6ft long stainless steel flip-top cigarette-type packet, loaded onto a lorry for transport to the Arnolfini Gallery in Bristol where it was opened with a circular saw to allow his escape. Following this, members of the audience were given 'a little craft guidance' in wielding mallets in order to help crush the empty packet. 'Watch the volunteers indulge in a craft activity' announced the catalogue. This had led on from an earlier performance in 1978 at the same venue in which the jeweller had had himself welded into a giant stainless steel tin can and released with a giant tin opener. Saddington stated he wanted to have 'an insight into the notion of getting inside a piece of jewellery to wear it.'

Twenty years since Arnolfini had been founded, its annual number of visitors had risen to over 150,000. The gross income in 1980-81 was £416,000, of which 35 per cent came from the Arts Council and 29 per cent from the restaurant and bar. During 1981, an exhibition by the Brotherhood of Ruralists was organised by Arnolfini and Camden Arts Centre, London. The Brotherhood had been formed in 1975 by a group of artists including Peter Blake, one of the most influential artists of Pop Art – in 1967, with his then wife Jann, he had designed the cover of the Beatles' album *Sergeant Pepper's Lonely Hearts Club Band*. Reviewing its two decades, Arnolfini's 1981 annual report stated: 'One of our most important objectives is the educative one of stimulating critical interest in, and arousing discussion of, the activities we present – which often leads to greater enjoyment of the work seen and heard. Performances are complemented by classes, workshops and weekend schools. Artists, conductors, composers, jewellers, directors and choreographers are given the opportunity to talk about their work. Audiences have the chance to challenge and discuss their explanations. 'Audience participation' is more than an abstract concept. At Arnolfini dance workshops, for example, people

Contemporary dance at Arnolfini: *Bella Copia*, 2002.

enjoy contact with visiting artists from this country and abroad – many with international reputations. Another aspect of Arnolfini policy is the presentation of mixed media events. Films are linked with exhibitions. Music is related to sculpture.'

Saturday morning workshops for children were always held, in liaison with art teachers at every level of education in the region. Art education at all ages was seen as a high priority. Jeremy Rees wrote: 'It was always considered that the whole Arnolfini programme (including the extensive bookshop and Arnolfini publications) was underpinned by a concern for 'life-long' education in the contemporary arts. Many of the exhibitions and live events were also programmed with accompanying talks, discussions and practical workshops with artists and performers.'

Sculpture trail

By 1983, the number of visitors to Arnolfini had risen to about 200,000 visitors a year and the exhibitions continued to attract much attention, not least in the media. 'Rees unrepentant about shock show,' headlined *Bristol Evening Post* in October that year. It was an exhibition of photographs by Robert Mapplethorpe which included portraits of Lord Snowdon and Debbie Harry but also, the *Post* stated, 'of men chums…in frankly erotic poses.' At the same time, there were paintings by Paula Rego which were described as her first major English public exhibition. Born in Portugal, she had studied at the Slade School of Fine Art. Joe Tilson, another prominent painter, was one of the exhibitors the following year, when Arnolfini initiated a new and lasting venture in collaboration with the Forestry Commission: the Forest of Dean Sculpture Trail in Gloucestershire.

The 3.5-mile trail is in Gloucestershire's ancient forest which had a history of charcoal making, coal mining and iron smelting. Along the pathways are about 20 permanent and temporary sculptures by leading sculptors such as Peter Randall-Page, Cornelia Parker and

Ian Hamilton Finlay. Martin Orrom of the Forestry Commission was the founder chair of Forest of Dean Sculpture Trust, with Jeremy a founder and lifelong trustee. Rupert Martin, author of *The Sculpted Forest*, which Bristol's Redcliffe Press published in 1990, and Arnolfini's co-ordinator when the trail was started, wrote that Orrom 'had the vision to see the potential of such a project, and the genius to bring together artists and foresters into a working partnership through the mediation of an art gallery.'

Arnolfini, however, was in financial turmoil. Although gross turnover in 1983-84 was £506,600, expenditure outstripped revenue. The Arts Council's grant was cut by one per cent to £193,000 and South West Arts' funding by one per cent to £21,000. The British Film Industry cut its grant by half to £6,000 and threatened to end it because of its commitment to support Watershed Media Centre, which had opened in 1982 in transit sheds converted by JT on St. Augustine's Reach. [*See* Chapter 8: Actions and ambitions.]

Bristol's *Venue* magazine reported that Arnolfini could lose its cinema, live performance programme and contemporary jewellery department. 'If this should occur it is almost inevitable that what remained would move out of its prestigious Bush House home and mark the demise of a centre which has pioneered an unparalleled concentration of the arts in the provinces.' *Venue* added: 'Avon County Council contributes nothing. Bristol City Council has recently increased its annual grant from £1,500 to £5,000 but its overall contribution is still meagre in proportion to the other funding organisations...If both Avon County Council and Bristol City Council between them contributed on the same level as South West Arts, the Arnolfini's funding crisis would be solved.'

It was a fraught time for Arnolfini, which had a staff of 36 full-time and part-time people, including nine who looked after the restaurant/bar. Several redundancies were made and Jeremy Rees wrote letters seeking support. *Bristol Evening Post* reported that 'beleaguered' Arnolfini received a reply from John Cope, the Tory MP for Northavon, saying that he couldn't support public funds for its cinema because its current programme included a foreign film about lesbians and another about incest.

In June, the city council gave one-off grants of £50,000 to Arnolfini and the same amount to Watershed Media Centre. Arnolfini survived but Peter Barker-Mill stood down as chair in 1985, when he was in his late 70s. The following year, when Arnolfini commemorated its first 25 years, he stated: 'I wish to record with admiration my long and happy relationship with Jeremy Rees, who conceived, founded and inspires Arnolfini.' During the quarter-century, more than 600 exhibitions had been displayed with over 1,000 artists. Peter wrote: 'It is upon the works of promising or recognised artists that Arnolfini depends, as equally upon the interest, support and involvement of the community, and all who visit us. Art programmes must be made ever more accessible, not diluted in terms of popularity, but presented with intent to provide introduction, to foster comprehension, to evoke appreciation and thus enrich the experience and enjoyment of those who come through our doors.'

Decision to go

During that 25th anniversary year of 1986, Jeremy Fry, a Bath-based entrepreneur, took over as chair from Peter. In the autumn, Jeremy Rees decided to resign. Funding had become what *Venue* described as 'the most dire financial crisis ever faced by the Arnolfini.' The Arts Council in 1984 had produced its report *The Glory of the Garden* to promote new funding strategies for the regional arts. Its policy backfired when it sought to have funding parity with Bristol City Council, hoping it would support the cultural organisation. The city council objected and the Arts Council withdrew an initial £50,000 from its grant to Arnolfini. The council chose not to make up the shortfall, with *Venue* reporting that it resulted in a 'formidable deficit.'

Venue quoted Jeremy Rees as saying, 'In all my time here, my one disappointment has been that the city and county have failed to make a realistic contribution to what has, in effect, been provided as a public service.' *Bristol Evening Post* reported that the two Jeremys had not agreed on the future direction of Arnolfini. 'J. Rees would like to see it remain as a flagship for the experimental, the new, the potential classics. J. Fry sees the need for the Arnolfini to pay more of its way and get out of the never-ending battles with a philistine council.'

When asked by *Venue* what qualities his successor should have, Jeremy Rees replied: 'Tenacity.' Barry Barker, previously director of exhibitions at the ICA and director of John Hansard Gallery at Southampton University, was appointed to succeed him in 1987, followed in 1991 by Tessa Jackson. Jeremy and Annabel moved to London and he became an arts management consultant. He advised Ipswich Borough Council on an enterprising scheme for a European visual arts centre to relate British with continental contemporary art. Rate-capped by central government, the council decided not to proceed with the project. He encouraged the use of information technology in museums and libraries and was a trustee of the Contemporary Art Society, which gives works to museums, and he remained a trustee of the Forest of Dean Sculpture Trust. Jeremy died in December 2003, aged 66, after being struck by a motorcycle when walking near the family's home in London. His mother Jean, who in 1989 was elected artists' chairman for the Royal West of England Academy for three years, died in 2004.

Caroline Collier, Arnolfini's director who succeeded Tessa Jackson in September 1999, described Jeremy Rees as 'a pioneer and a visionary", who was 'a role model for arts administrators as seers and enablers...In shaping Arnolfini, Rees enacted his qualities, creating an institution that was openminded, generous, imaginative, principled, independent and, above all, fast moving and radical.' The Forest of Dean Sculpture Trust said it was 'indebted to Jeremy for his commitment and enthusiasm which has seen the trust become one of the most prestigious sculpture trails in the world.' Mel Gooding, in an obituary in *The Guardian*, wrote: 'A deeply cultured and intellectually curious man, Rees was a boundlessly animateur of genius. He was also a man in whom the values of a decent concern for others ran deep. He inspired great affection among staff, artists and performers, who recognised a friend and ally, and a lover of all things creative.'

Nicholas Serota, director of Tate, wrote that Jeremy had been an 'inspirational director.' Arnolfini, he stated, 'set the pace outside London in the quality of its collaboration with artists and in the range of its activities…For those of us working outside London in the 1970s, Jeremy was the prime example of someone who showed how to realise a bold vision with an unusual combination of conviction, personal charm and persistence…He was far ahead of his time.'

8 Actions and ambitions
The business evolves

Architecture and building are only concerned with creating a built environment
which is beautiful and solid, agreeable, habitable and decent.
Léon Krier, architect (b. 1946)

JT, before it moved to Bush House, widened its ambitions in 1973 when Britain, having switched to decimal currency in 1971, introduced value-added tax and finally joined the European Economic Community. JT Building Group, the holding company, was changed to JT Group 'to reflect the fundamental changes in its activities.' Its operating structure changed to three divisions: construction, development and leisure.

Residential development had been an important part of the business but was dwindling as the national economy deteriorated after the quadrupled oil prices. The company, seeking to balance the cyclical earnings of its building activities, diversified into the leisure and sports-based hotel industry to broaden its base. Millgrange Holdings, a property development company, merged with JT to add, John Pontin stated, 'a completely new dimension to our development operations.' David Perry, who had been associated with JT since the Harley Court development, and Bill Trump, who had been JT's solicitor from 1961 onwards, became non-executive directors.

This was to launch JT's new leisure division. Ashton Court Country Club had been founded by John Ley who then bought St Pierre Golf & Country Club which had been created by Bill Graham. John Pontin was then invited in January 1973 to be a non-executive director of the Ashton Court group. Ashton Court was set in 15 acres near Bristol, and St Pierre Golf & Country Club with 400 acres near Chepstow, Wales. JT acquired in August 1973 the two country clubs which were developed as hotels for short-break fitness and leisure stays, a relatively unknown business concept in the UK. Ashton Court – to be renamed Redwood Lodge – was described by JT as 'probably the largest facility of its kind in Europe with 17 squash courts, six badminton courts, 18 snooker tables and three swimming pools.' St Pierre, with a house dating back to the fourteenth century, was developed with 74 bedrooms, two golf courses, two badminton courts, five squash courts and an indoor pool.

The brewers Whitbread became partners in 1974 with JT's newly-formed leisure division by acquiring 32.5 per cent of Ashton Court. Whitbread subscribed for additional shares to provide finance to develop Ashton Court and St Pierre, and then to create other clubs from scratch. The joint venture, named Country Club Hotels, was expanded with investments in South Marston at Swindon, Tewkesbury Park in Gloucestershire and Meon Valley, near Southampton. The Country Club Hotels' brochure stated: 'We have extensive leisure facilities on hand for the energetic and comfort in abundance for those who would rather relax at their leisure.'

In undertaking the Country Club Hotels, eight of which were to be built between 1974 and 1989, JT demonstrated that it could design and build complicated and highly serviced structures as well as simpler commercial and industrial projects. Identified with the leisure industry, the company gained a high profile, encouraging potential clients to recognise that its fixed-price approach and tight programming could result in better value for money than conventional procurement methods. John, in his chairman's report in November 1974, stated: 'Turnover remains firmly based on our design and build service, with its well-established benefits of economy and speed. We have found that in difficult economic conditions, building owners become even more determined to seek a service that gives value for money, while maintaining high architectural standards…Viewing the future, I believe that as a result of overcoming the country's current economic problems there will be more leisure and not less.'

Staverton Contractors

It was during 1975, when the conversion of Bush House was completed, that the company took over Staverton Contractors which was owned by Dartington Hall Trust in South Devon, and the subsidiary Dartington Plant, which was to be subsequently sold in 1979. Staverton, a long-established and traditional contracting company, had fallen into serious financial difficulties during the national recession. It was grossly undercapitalised. The deal included Dartington Hall taking an 18 per cent shareholding in JT and with Christopher Zealley, Director and a Trustee of Dartington, joining the board.

John described the takeover as adding 'a unique dimension to our group' and which was to cause a much closer relationship with Dartington for years to come [as shown in the next two chapters.] The immediate aim was to try to reorganise Staverton into a design and build operation and several of its contracts were carried out using JT's in-house design team, while Staverton's directors John Clements and George Wyatt contributed to the group's overall expertise.

JT Design and Build

JT's many design and build projects included Gateway supermarkets, depots for UBM builders' merchants and several town halls. Opportunities in the public sector had risen from the 1972 Local Government Act which required the reorganisation of councils

Avon Way, Bristol
for Millgrange
Properties Ltd.

throughout England and Wales except in London. New county councils were formed, with
Avon in 1974 encompassing Bristol and its surrounding region. Competitive design and
build tenders were won for town halls, swimming pools and other public buildings. The
company was involved early in the university science park movement, with the master
planning and building of the first phase of Southampton's Chilworth Park. Other
university work included the teaching and research facility of the department of
pharmacology at Cambridge. Roger Mortimer noted: 'This important project had stalled
due to the high building costs of the scheme designed by a private architect – a not
uncommon reason for JT's introduction. Our complete redesign met all clients' needs at 20
per cent less cost and was completed ahead of schedule – a pleasant change in university
projects.'

In the private sector, the Durdhamside and Chartley flats built in Bristol were commended by the Civic Trust, which stated its awards were given 'to outstanding examples of
architecture and environmental design and are unique in that they take into account the
benefit each project brings to its local area, as well as considering the quality of its design.'
Awards for 'Good design in housing' from the Department of the Environment included
the Bristol scheme of High Kingsdown, which also won a prize from the European Housing
Institute.

Corporate Development

David Johnstone, of Thomson McLintock, became involved with JT because of two of its problems: Tim Organ's shares had been acquired 'out of cashflow' using the company's own money to buy the shares, and the redevelopment of the Old Bristol Pottery. John had contracted to buy the pottery site on a deferred contract and had been unable in the time to finance the scheme.

'We had a partners' meeting to decide whether to take on this rather racy client, whom I thought that we should support,' David remembered. 'John promised never to commit himself like that again (which he did not do) and I introduced him to Peter Gerrard at Lovell White & King [the law firm] who resolved the legal issue relating to the shares, and an introduction to London Life provided a solution to the Pottery site. Thereafter John instantly absorbed the idea of good corporate governance and I would argue that the group (initially it was a collection of companies under common ownership) was run better than many public companies with regular board meetings, printed annual accounts, schemes to create an internal market in shares with employee trusts, a final salary pension scheme and encouragement of individual employee share ownership.'

David became JT's audit partner and developed a financial advisory function, and Jack Sowersby (subsequently recruited from Thomson McLintock as group accountant) became audit manager. Tim Miles (current group accountant and company secretary) was also to be drawn from that firm. Bill Trump, aided by Nick Pritchard, handled the property matters and David Gray, of Lovell White & King, became the lead corporate lawyer. The financial and legal functions were greatly improved. David Johnstone commented: 'The business model was extremely cash generative with payments from customers being received well before payment to suppliers (many of whom were on annually negotiated contracts). This was the time of stock relief because of rampant inflation and the group benefited from a very low tax charge. The funds generated could be used to finance the development programme.'

Overseas projects

JT's first overseas projects were a consequence of the recession which had caused architects and construction companies to search for international work. JT followed that trend and during 1975 it set up a joint venture called Arabuild, in partnership with the Al Mulla group, to win contracts in Dubai. The venture, with an expatriate team led by Des Williams and assisted by staff from JT and Staverton Contractors, got off to an encouraging start with £9m of contracts, 'demonstrating that a medium-sized contractor, with the right local partner, can share in this enormous construction market,' John Pontin stated.

The company's schemes in the UK were led in the company's usual informal manner by

Roger Mortimer and Howard Williams. Project management and technical personnel included Harry Mellor and Richard Demery, supported by Roger Averis and Mike Peel. As with other construction companies, it was men rather than women who would be recruited to senior positions. Some firms would advertise for men only: two advertisements in the *Architects' Journal* in 1975: 'We need a man in his late twenties, skilled in the design of house and estate layouts, to lead a small design team' and another company wanted a 'keen and enthusiastic young man' as an architect.

Group turnover rose in the year to April 1978 from £7.8m to £13.6m and to £16.3m in the following year. The closing decade was still turbulent with the Labour government in jeopardy after the 'winter of discontent' of industrial pay strikes and rising inflation. Despite this uncertain period, John stated in January 1979 that 'for the first time in several years we are able to look forward to a more prosperous period in the UK. Our level of turnover in the current year is substantially up on last year.' The construction division had come through a 'difficult period of low turnover' and was now in 'its strongest position for several years. The bulk of the turnover has again been in factories, warehouses and shops.'

John reported that the Arabuild joint venture 'made a substantial contribution to the year's results and, after the accounting year-end, paid a dividend of approximately three times our original investment.' Several large contracts were completed, the most notable being the marble-clad Dubai Municipality Building which was not designed by JT but by Japanese architects. It was built in 1978 and officially opened by Queen Elizabeth. 'While it is the case that the volume of work in the United Arab Emirates is slackening off,' John said, 'our partners in the Middle East are anxious to expand our operations. And we are taking active steps to explore the international market.'

With the Middle East's oil boom ending in 1979, the chairman reported that Arabuild's 'construction activity has fallen away to practically nothing…however, this rundown in activity overseas has freed valuable personnel who return to the UK in time to meet our increasing workload here.' His report added: 'We are undertaking with our partners in the Middle East and a US corporation a joint development in Florida with a Municipality Building, Dubai, built by Arabuild Ltd.

view to testing the market there.' But JT's initiative in Florida, investing in a leisure residential development by subscribing for 45 per cent of the equity in Nash-JT Inc., in association with Nash-Ellsworth International, was to prove unsuccessful and costly. It was eventually unwound.

Political change

In Britain, a turning point came in May 1979 when Margaret Thatcher led the Conservatives to victory over the Labour government. Despite the revenues flowing from North Sea oil – the huge Forties field had been discovered in 1970 and was followed by other finds – the economy was struggling with a balance of payments' deficit, price inflation and high interest rates. Thatcher, rejecting the post-war consensus politics, introduced monetarist policies for what she called an 'enterprise economy'. There was a sharp rise in unemployment and inner cities began to disintegrate with a riot at St. Paul's in Bristol and a 'long hot summer' of riots in other cities.

JT itself was prospering. 'The construction division has had another record year and remains the mainstay of the group,' John Pontin reported in November 1980. The division's subsidiaries were now named JT Design Build, incorporating Building Partnership (Bristol), and Staverton Contractors. John added that 'a great deal of time and money has been spent on the hotel side of our leisure division in creating the appropriate infrastructure of rooms and conference suites. It is currently trading at levels above the national average.'

The broad range of professional staff included the architects Bob Hunt and Mike Duckering, together with John Ellis and Richard Needs. The technical ability of the design staff was rising to meet the requirements of more sophisticated contracts. Much structural design was carried out in-house with key staff at that time being Mike Boyce and Bob Evans. The in-house building services engineers were responsible for setting performance standards for installation contractors. Land surveying, graphic design and landscape skills were also employed. Computer-aided design was introduced for architectural drafting and computerised systems were used for estimating and surveying, while buying staff would meet the project teams' requirements from the initial inquiries through to job completion. Quantity surveyors commissioned by clients showed their appreciation of JT's clear and accurate cost breakdowns.

Among the Staverton Contractors' projects in the early 1980s were a studio and workshops for Television South West and two schools, Cockington Junior School at Torquay and Torquay Boys Grammar School which had 750 pupils. These were conventional contracts designed by independent architects employed by the client. Under JT's ownership Staverton's design and build service started well, with a major car components factory in Plymouth and offices in Bethnal Green, London, for the Institute of Community Studies. But the culture of a long established and traditional building company proved a barrier to a wholehearted conversion to design and build.

In contrast, JT continued to innovate with JT Design Build introducing 'volumetric' factory-built room modules to convert The Grange restaurant, near Bristol, to a 32-bedroomed hotel. The system, innovative in the UK, had been adopted in Sweden and the US for student accommodation, budget hotels and low-cost housing. These modules were developed by JT, with the assistance of the Timber Research & Development Association, and previously used at the group's Ashton Court Hotel & Country Club. The hotel bedroom and bathroom 'boxes', fully finished, were delivered to the site and craned into position on simple foundations. They were then connected to services and roofed and externally clad with materials chosen to be appropriate to the local environment.

This method provided very short building periods and guaranteed factory standards of finish. John Pontin and Roger Mortimer had been both impressed with the benefits of engineered timber-frame construction on their visits to Scandinavia and the US. The ease with which high insulation could be achieved and the environmentally friendly nature of timber construction were further attractions. A similar volumetric method was adopted by several large manufacturers and hotel groups in future decades.

Watershed Media Centre

The acclaimed restoration of Bush House influenced Bristol City Council to abandon its intention to demolish the Floating Harbour's transit sheds for redevelopment of the redundant docklands. Many local people campaigned to keep the waterfront's character by finding new uses for the sheds – the E-shed was particularly admired for its decorated gable-end in St. Augustine's Reach. E and W-sheds, leased by JT from the city council, were converted by JT in a £1.6m scheme linking the two sheds to create Watershed Media Centre. Robert Trapnell, the project architect, achieved the complex spatial and technical requirements without major new structures. He also chose its name and logo.

Watershed, opened in 1982, was the first of its kind in the country to promote media creativity and innovation, showing independent films, hosting film festivals and related educational programmes. JT assisted the under-financed Watershed, helping to find funding and taking a generous approach at times of financial pressure. It was to become an important cultural venue with its cinemas and café-restaurant, complementing Arnolfini across the water and together drawing ever more visitors to the waterfront. It sees itself as 'a facilitator, a hub and a catalyst within the creative industries,' working with organisations in creative activity including Aardman Animations which, founded in Bristol in 1972, became famous for 'Wallace and Gromit' films and winning Oscars. The British Film

Arnolfini in W-Shed, 1973.

Institute has said that 'Watershed is not only a regional model of excellence, but a venue of national importance to which cinema programmers and venue directors across Britain can look for inspiration.'

The sheds were also the home for café-bars and Radio West, which had won the local independent radio franchise and went on air in 1981. The radio station was chaired by Glynne Wickham, Marmaduke Hussey (the former chief executive of Times Newspapers and later chairman of the BBC) and then by John Pontin. Financially-struggling, Radio West merged in 1985 with Wiltshire Radio, forming GWR which was based at Watershed. (In 1987, GWR became a publicly quoted company and is now a part of GCap Media plc)

The sympathetically converted redundant sheds proved to be another excellent exemplar of sustainable redevelopment. JT, which also leased the U and V-sheds which staged Bristol Exhibition Centre, planned to convert the sheds as Expo Bristol, a £4m scheme in a new hall to be capable of having indoor tennis matches watched by 1,000 people. The company saw the plan as 'the next piece in the jigsaw of redeveloping the historic harbour.' The scheme, though, did not proceed because of the council's planning uncertainties over potential developments.

Privatised industries

Margaret Thatcher had boosted her popularity when in 1982 the armed forces recaptured the Falkland Islands after the invasion by Argentine troops, and the next year, the Conservatives won the June general election by a landslide. Anthony Sampson, in *The*

Changing Anatomy of Britain (1983) wrote: 'The re-election of Thatcher after four years of recession and high unemployment undoubtedly signalled a major change in the British political mood after the 1960s and 1970s – a preference for the kind of authoritarian and uncomfortable government which would have been unthinkable in the climate of high expectations and permissiveness under Wilson or even Heath.' The government carried out a radical programme of privatisation of nationalised industries – British Telecom was privatised in 1984 – as well as the sale of council houses and the reform of industrial relations.

JT, during the financial year to April 1983, reported that the company had 'successfully demonstrated our ability to complete larger and more complex work and this has culminated in winning a major office and high tech development at Cambridge. At some £12m it is our largest UK contract yet.' That year, JT formed a joint company, Sheraton-JT, with Sheraton Securities International, a property investment company quoted on the Unlisted Securities Market. JT Group itself never chose to become a publicly quoted company although, in its early years, this had been visualised as a possibility. Had it done so, it would have become a very different organisation, brought under the influence of institutional investors and the volatility of the stock market.

'As a private company we have been able to take a longer view of all our activities than might have been possible as a quoted company under the pressure of short-term fluctuations in share price,' John said in December 1983. 'This year has seen a substantial reorganisation of the group's structure and a movement in certain activities away from direct involvement through subsidiaries to joint ventures through associated companies. In the development area, this move enables us to share in larger schemes than any we could undertake on our own behalf. Similar moves in our leisure division leave the UK design and build construction operations more clearly identified as the mainstay of the group's trading profits.' He added that JT Design Build had increased its turnover by more than 20 per cent over the previous year, 'with by far the largest contribution coming from the London and Greater London area. This is an outstanding performance in view of the recession which has faced all builders.'

Within the construction industry, design and build companies were still regarded as controversial but benefited from a report by the National Economic Development Council (*Faster Building for Industry*, HMSO, 1983). Its case studies assessed the comparative performance of the different methods of organisation. Traditional construction companies were assessed for total project times on industrial buildings at being 25 per cent fast, 29 per cent average and 46 per cent slow. Design and build companies were assessed at 47 per cent fast, 21 per cent average and 32 per cent slow. The report concluded: 'Fast building is possible without sacrificing either cost or quality.'

While the year 1984 was not as grim as George Orwell's foreboding 'Big Brother' novel *1984* (published in 1949), it was a time of extreme political and industrial conflict when miners went on strike after the National Coal Board announced the closure of many coalpits. The dispute, led by Arthur Scargill of the National Union of Mineworkers, was a direct challenge to the Thatcher government. It became one of the most violent confrontations between the miners' pickets and the police yet seen in England. In October, the government faced a direct act of terrorism when the IRA bombed the Grand Hotel in Brighton where the prime minister and Conservative ministers were staying during a party conference. Five people were killed. The IRA had been murdering civilians in England with bombs planted in public places since the early 1970s. Eventually, the miners' strike collapsed and Thatcher's image as an 'Iron Lady' was maintained.

It was during 1984 that the activities of JT's Arabuild joint venture with the Al Mulla group had been wound down. 'This brings to a conclusion a happy and profitable ten-year partnership with the Al Mulla family in Dubai,' John stated. During the financial year 1985-86, group turnover reached a record £38m and the value of on-site contracts for JT Design Build and Staverton Contractors was over £75m.

25 years completed

In 1986, the London stock market was deregulated as the 'Big Bang', with member firms able to operate as brokers and dealers in a dual capacity and taking transactions away from the stock exchange floor to telephones and computers in separate dealing rooms. By then, JT had completed its first 25 years, having fulfilled over 250 design and build contracts on a lump-sum, fixed-price basis, including many repeat orders. Most of its contracts were in southern England, many in the Bristol region and in London. They ranged from Truro in Cornwall, Plymouth and Bournemouth on the south coast, Tunbridge Wells in Kent, Colchester in Essex, and Norwich and King's Lynn in Norfolk. In central southern England, there were projects in Reading, Swindon, Birmingham, Oxford and Cambridge; in Wales, in Cardiff and Carmarthen. There were a few projects further north, including Manchester, Sheffield and Rotherham.

The company's spectrum of work had encompassed virtually every kind of building: houses and flats, offices, hotels, sports and leisure clubs, swimming pools, arts spaces including cinemas, council offices, churches, airport buildings, university facilities, supermarkets and shopping precincts, factories, industrial buildings and warehouses. By this time JT had long-term relationships with several clients which allowed the efficiencies of design and build, from site appraisal to fitted-out buildings, to develop further.

John commented: 'To me the years have passed very quickly, partly because so many of my colleagues have been involved from very early days in JT's growth from the smallest of

Bristol contractors into a major force in construction, spearheading a substantial and diverse group.' Marking its 25th anniversary, JT stated: 'To attract and retain good people, a company must create the right environment in all respects. From the outset, JT has had its own special culture, based on informality, flexibility and positive encouragement to take responsibility. This has created a climate where corporate loyalty is strong, and hard work is both a way of life and enjoyable.' It added: 'The early ideals of a design conscious construction service giving value for money, combined with single source responsibility are as valid today as they were then. The company's pioneering design and build philosophy, imitated in recent years by major construction companies, has proved itself time after time. Fixed price contracts, single source responsibility, and savings of time and money are increasingly attractive in today's complex and competitive market.'

Roger Mortimer, reviewing the group's quarter-century, commented: 'It had been hard work with a full share of problems, but JT had become firmly recognised as one of the very few specialist design and build contractors of repute. The early years had been times of almost constant innovation and development. Now the pace of change had understandably slowed, reflecting in part the way the industry had moved towards acceptance of design and build as an approach. But much of the creative early thinking had been absorbed into a JT culture. The most important element of that culture was the enthusiasm, hard work and fierce loyalty of key people at all levels. Some of this was undoubtedly due to the conviction that the JT way of doing things was "right".'

Community matters

John Pontin became less involved in the everyday management of JT Design Build as he concentrated on other group interests, as well as his long-standing involvement in community and charitable matters. As a consequence of his own working-class inner-city background, he had strong convictions that the lack of academic further education should not be a barrier to careers. The company ran a training scheme for school-leavers, involving hands-on experience, plus part-time college courses. Most of the annual intake responded well and found a useful role in their chosen area of work. Some were to have long and successful careers with the company, becoming senior managers. Two of these were Roger Averis and Mike Peel who became directors of JT Design Build.

The group's contribution to the community was mainly given to locally based charities. 'On the arts front, our major support has been to Arnolfini and to the Watershed Arts Trust,' the company stated. 'In sports, support through sponsorship and practical assistance has gone to squash and badminton as well as soccer, rugby and cricket.' After Erin Pizzey founded the first refuge for battered wives in 1971, other refuges were set up around the country and Women's Aid, which ran a house in Bristol, had thanked John and the JT

Group 'who have made it possible for our work to continue in this country.' The Greater Bristol Foundation, to act as a link between local donors and local needs, was set up in 1987 with John involved in its formation by the Society of Merchant Venturers and JT providing initial office space. The foundation (now named Quartet Community Foundation) has since distributed over £7m in grants to voluntary and community groups. John, a trustee of the foundation, became a patron of Bristol's Hartcliffe Community Campus. He was also chairman of Bristol 1000 Community Trust which, in January 1987, published its first business newsletter, called The Associate. 'The objectives of the trust', its editorial stated, 'are ones we believe businessmen throughout the county endorse: the stimulation of economic activity and employment; the provision of good quality work experience and training for young people.'

At this time John was also involved with UK 2000, a partnership of seven voluntary organisations under the chairmanship of Richard Branson and private-sector board members, including John. Its government-funded work ranged from greening cities and restoring industrial heritage to tourist projects. Thatcher said it was 'to generate quality environmental improvement schemes and to raise business awareness of the environment.' Thatcher retained power in June 1987 with a big parliamentary majority. It was in October that year that the country suffered unpredicted environmental damage: the 'Great Storm.' Believed to be the worst storm since 1703, it struck south-east England, causing severe damage to buildings and the destruction of many millions of trees.

9 The Dartington Hall connection
How JT became intimately linked

You read everywhere, in every paper you turn to, that the individual is being killed by our mechanistic and technological society. That is not true at Dartington – the individual here is still very, very important, thank heaven!
Dorothy Elmhirst, Foundation Day speech, June 1960

For three decades, there has been a close connection between JT Group and Dartington Hall, the unique combination of educational, business and cultural endeavours on a rural estate of about 850 acres, set in the curve of the River Dart near Totnes in South Devon.

The enterprises and the estate – an evocative mixture of medieval and modern buildings, landscaped gardens with sculptures, farmland and forest – are owned by Dartington Hall Trust. The relationship began in 1975 when JT took over Staverton Contractors which, founded and owned by Dartington, had become one of the largest private construction companies in the South-west. The connection, though, was to become much more embracing than the corporate control of Staverton Contractors. Five years after the acquisition, in 1980 John Pontin became a Dartington trustee and then in 1994 its chairman, while Dartington, retaining a substantial minority shareholding in JT, has stayed represented on the group's board.

Dartington Hall itself dated from 1388 when the manor and courtyard were built for John Holand, Earl of Huntingdon and whose crest – a white hart on a red rose – is to be seen on a stone archway. He was beheaded after a failed rebellion and Dartington changed hands until it was acquired in 1559 by Sir Arthur Champernowne, a vice-admiral. Sir Arthur's successors lived at Dartington for over 300 years but the property was largely derelict after the First World War. It was bought in 1925 by Leonard and Dorothy Elmhirst, who had the money and determination to put their idealistic concepts into practice.

Leonard was born in 1893 into a land-owning family in Yorkshire, although the estate had been much reduced and his father, a parson, received income mainly from licensing the coalfields under his land. Medically unfit for military service, Leonard left Cambridge University and went to India where he undertook agricultural work with a British missionary, Sam Higginbottom. In 1919 he went to Cornell University in the US to study modern farming techniques which could be adopted in India. While he was president of the students' union at Cornell, he met Dorothy. Born in 1887, she was a daughter of the multi-millionaire William C. Whitney (Gertrude Vanderbilt, who wed an older brother of

Dorothy, founded the Whitney Museum of American Art) Dorothy married the diplomat Willard Straight in 1911 and they lived in China before returning to New York. By then they had three children and so a new house was built for them on Fifth Avenue. Although from an immensely privileged background, Dorothy actively supported radical organisations, financing the New School for Social Research in New York while her husband was a founder of *The New Republic* magazine, still published today.

English experiment

During the First World War, Willard Straight served in France but died in 1918 during the influenza pandemic. Dorothy, after meeting Leonard, decided to finance a student union building at Cornell as a memorial to her husband who had attended the university. Leonard, while in New York, also met Rabindranath Tagore, the Indian poet and social reformer who had won a Nobel Prize for literature. Leonard graduated from Cornell in 1921 and returned to India where he worked on Tagore's estate in West Bengal, setting up a department of rural reconstruction. He wrote a village school prospectus, stating that the purpose of education was: 'To release the imagination, to give it wings, to 'open wide the mind's caged door', this is the most vital service that it is in the power of one human being to render to another.' This credo and his experience in India were to be the cornerstone of what was to be an 'English experiment', following Tagorean ideals.

Dorothy's warmth towards Leonard had grown, despite misgivings among her family, and when he returned to England from India they met and became engaged. Together, planning the 'English experiment', they needed 'a place'. Leonard told the estate agents Knight, Frank & Rutley what they wanted: 'It must be beautiful, we're starting a school. We expect to make farming pay. It must have a reasonably productive soil and climate, and as much variety as possible, woods, forest, orchards etc. And if you can give me all those, then historical associations thrown in. Yes, and in Devon, Dorset or Somerset.' The agents had 48 estates on offer in the West Country and Leonard, with his sister, drove from London to Devon in March 1925. After dismissing Syon Abbey near South Brent as 'dull', they came to the Dartington Hall estate. Knight, Frank & Rutley described it as 'the historical freehold residential, agricultural property including the historic mansion of Dartington Hall' as well as 'two capital dairy farms, in good heart' and 'several country cottages.' Leonard wrote to Dorothy that it was a 'veritable fairyland', even though it was in decay with the medieval building, the Great Hall, roofless and windowless.

A month later, after securing an option on the property, the couple married, he aged 31 and she 38. On their return from honeymoon, the purchase was negotiated for £30,000. Repairs and reconstruction began, supervised by the architect William Weir. Leonard instigated novel farming and forestry projects to create employment in the impoverished

Dartington Hall, an evocative mixture of medieval and modern, home of the Dartington Hall Trust.

countryside, while Dorothy believed that the arts must be an intrinsic part of their initiatives. They started the school as early as 1926 with a stable block converted to a boarding house. 'Its central idea,' wrote William Curry, who became its headmaster in 1930, 'is that the new world will be created not by politicians, but by men and women of goodwill, in large and small groups throughout the world, undertaking the task of creation, wherever their influence extends.'

It was always to be a small fee-paying school, needing additional financial support by the trust, but it was intended to be 'free' or progressive, unlike conventional British schools. Dorothy was appalled by the anecdotal accounts of perpetual bullying at English public schools. Leonard himself had not enjoyed his time at Repton. 'In comparison with most schools we offer children a great deal of personal freedom,' a Dartington prospectus said. Pupils were of either sex, wearing their own clothes and not uniforms. There were no dormitories – each student having his or her own bedroom – and a minimum of rules with no prefects and no punishments. While academic goals were high, classroom work was never enforced rigidly. Pupils learned practical skills by working alongside the farmers and estate workers.

By the early 1930s, Dartington was an agricultural estate with modernised farms,

The Elmhirsts of Dartington, idealism and foresight.

poultry enterprises and an artificial insemination centre – one of the first in Britain. Orchards were planted, with a cider-making and fruit-juice press. A sawmill and furniture factory were established while commercial woodlands were extended as far as Dartmoor. Artists, potters, musicians and craftsmen were coming to Dartington, making it buzz with excitement and activity. Bernard Leach set up a pottery workshop which became established as Dartington Pottery. Some of the artists and performers came as refugees from Nazi Germany, including the Russian-born Rudolf Laban, a pioneer of contemporary dance and who lectured at the Jooss-Leeder dance school at Dartington – Kurt Jooss and his ballet company were also refugees. The Russian actor Michael Chekhov initiated a theatre studio. The school began to attract international students and its premises were moved out from the courtyard to a new building, Foxhole.

Staverton started

A large force of skilled labourers restored the ruined buildings and built whatever new was needed. For some years the workforce was directly employed by the Elmhirsts. When the work on the estate lessened, Staverton Builders – Staverton is a village close to the estate – was set up and financed by the Elmhirsts as a privately owned firm which they later transferred into the trust. This was the company (to become Staverton Contractors) which, four decades later, was to be taken over by JT Group. Its first managing director, A.E. Malbon, had been general manager of Welwyn Builders, working on the creation of Welwyn Garden City after the First World War. Louis de Soissons, who had been in charge of designing the garden city, was the architect of housing for Dartington's workers, with some 45 properties being built by Staverton Contractors. The company's wider remit, as it began work elsewhere in the county, was to employ local labour, stimulate the rural economy and, together with Dartington's other businesses, to provide income for the many cultural activities. The village of Dartington was itself growing steadily, with the number of houses rising from about 125 in the 1920s to nearly 500 by 1970.

High Cross House, the Modernist home for the headmaster of Dartington School and

Bernard Leach in the pottery workshop at Dartington Hall.

designed by William Lescaze, was built in 1932 by Staverton Contractors. The blue and white house – two rectilinear blocks joined by a curved form – was in deliberate contrast to the Great Hall to emphasise that architecture should not merely imitate the past. Lescaze planned the interior finishes and furnishings in Modernist style with furniture made at Dartington. A *Country Life* article about the house, published in 1933, quoted the headmaster Curry: 'To me, serenity, clarity and a kind of openness are its distinguishing features.' The article added: 'The general contractors, who also executed all the fixed furniture and woodwork, were the local firm of Staverton Builders, who have shown themselves capable of working efficiently to strange specifications.' (High Cross House was converted in 1995 as a home to the trust's collection and archive.)

Lescaze also designed school buildings and purpose-built premises were constructed for performance arts, studios and workshops. Other architects who worked at Dartington included Oswald Milne and Walter Gropius, the Bauhaus architect who converted the

High Cross House, Dartington. Designed by William Lescaze and built by Staverton Contractors, 1932.

original tithe barn into the Barn Theatre. 'Dorothy and Leonard were private patrons of architecture on a grand scale, responsible for the largest collection of privately-funded buildings in England in this century,' claimed Michael Young, in his book *The Elmhirsts of Dartington* (Routledge & Kegan Paul, 1982), and who was one of the first pupils at Dartington Hall School. Young became the most prominent social innovator of the 20th century – Anthony Sampson, author of *The Changing Anatomy of Britain* (Hodder & Stoughton, 1983), described him as 'the prophet of the meritocracy'. Young had arrived at the school in 1929 at the age of 15, after miserable experiences at other schools. He was one of several children whom Dorothy and Leonard took into their own home, a kindness which he never forgot.

The diaspora of enterprises required more organisation, causing the Elmhirsts' advisers in 1935 to merge trusts and companies, including Staverton Contractors, into a charitable trust structure. Fears about the Nazi events in Germany caused the advisers to rearrange and protect Dorothy's fortune. The trust was allowed by the Charity Commission to hold and operate trading companies within a novel concept, probably unique at the time, called 'The General Scheme'. The provision of work for the local rural community was integral to Leonard's wish to make Dartington an economic as well as a cultural and educational enterprise. His concept could be called holistic, the enterprises being within a single coherent structure. In the early 1970s he expounded these ideas in a television documentary about Dartington, entitled 'A Job is Not Enough'. The Charity Commission at that time felt able to endorse what was a larger vision than the strict interpretation of the limits of charity work. This concept of a harmonious bridge between businesses and charitable activities of social value was to appeal to John Pontin.

New ventures

Dartington attracted world-renowned musicians and artists and continued to do so. They have included Benjamin Britten, John Cage, Imogen Holst, Peter Pears, Elisabeth Schumann, Ravi Shankar, Igor Stravinsky, John Tavener, Peter Maxwell Davies and Michael Tippett. The Amadeus String Quartet was formed there in 1948 after its European Jewish musicians came to England and the Elmhirsts provided them with quality instruments. Their chamber music became internationally admired for nearly 40 years until the quartet was dissolved in 1987. The Summer School of Music, founded at Bryanston, moved to Dartington in 1953 at Dorothy Elmhirst's invitation. William Glock, the BBC's controller of music and the founder of the Summer School, described it as a 'lifeline, not a sideline' because of the scope it gave to new work and talent. The arts department evolved into the College of Arts, which by the early 1960s emerged as an integrated structure for teaching music, modern dance, theatre and art.

Two new ventures began in the late 1960s when the trustees responded to the depressed economy in north Devon, which was suffering from a lack of employment and cultural activities in its large but thinly populated area. The idea of a glassworks was conceived by trustee Peter Sutcliffe and his friend Euan Cooper-Willis, who with his wife Susan began Portmeirion Pottery. A past pupil of the school, Susan was the daughter of Clough Williams-Ellis, the designer of Portmeirion village in north Wales. Sutcliffe recruited the first managing director, Eskil Vilhemson, from a Swedish glass manufacturer and he brought a team of Swedish craftsmen to Devon. Dartington Glass, as it was called (now Dartington Crystal), was opened at Torrington in 1967 with 12 Swedish skilled blowers and 17 local employees as trainee blowers and office staff. It had difficult early years while glass-blowing skills had to be taught to the local employees, working to Scandinavian and then British designs which did not sell. But Frank Thrower, the designer and marketing director, eventually became successful with the glassware throughout the UK and abroad. Within three years of its launch, the company won the Duke of Edinburgh's Award for design. Dartington Glass gained additional revenue by being a pioneer in attracting tourists to a working factory.

To launch the second project in north Devon, a large house was bought in the village of Beaford to become a new kind of arts centre. The Beaford Centre, as it was called, was devised and led by John Lane, an artist and writer. Using the house more as a base than a centre, Beaford promoted classes, a theatre company, a photographic archive and events around the villages in north Devon, all part of an imaginative scheme to enrich the social life of people living in the countryside.

Another innovation in the 1960s was the Social Research Unit, founded at King's College, Cambridge, by Royston Lambert to study public schools for a Royal Commission and then residential child care. It moved to Dartington in 1968 and Lambert became head of Dartington Hall School the following year. 'The new head had charm, fluency and, above all, ideas which flowed as freely as from Bill Curry in his prime,' wrote Young in his biography of the Elmhirsts. The Warren House Group, named after its headquarters in a Modernist building on Dartington's estate, evolved from the work of the research unit.

Changes at the Hall

Dorothy Elmhirst died in 1968, aged 81. Leonard remarried in 1972; Susanna Isaacs, a child psychiatrist, had been one of the early pupils at the school. He resigned as chairman when they decided to live in Los Angeles where Susanna had been offered a post at the University of Southern California. He died in 1974, aged 80. 'Together,' Young wrote of Dorothy and Leonard, 'they tried to give substance to a vision of the abundant life, in which the values of learning, community, worthwhile jobs and sound business practice might be balanced and combined.'

Young, who had been appointed a Dartington trustee in his twenties and was supported in much of his work by the Elmhirsts during their lifetimes, must have expected to be asked to succeed Leonard as chairman. He was already a national figure. He had drafted the Labour Party's radical post-war election manifesto and, during the 1950s, wrote his highly influential books *Family and Kinship in East London* (with the co-author Peter Willmott) and *The Rise of the Meritocracy*. He was a prime mover in the founding in 1957 of the Consumers' Association, which began product tests in a Bethnal Green converted garage and launched the publication of *Which?* magazine. Subsequently, he promoted the distance-learning concept of the Open University to Harold Wilson, then prime minister, and Jennie Lee, the government's first arts minister. The university had its first students in 1971. The two politicians took the credit for the Open University and offered Young no role in its establishment. James Callaghan, when prime minister, later offered Young the consolation of a peerage.

In the event, the Dartington trustees chose Maurice Ash as chairman, who had himself been a trustee since 1964. Ash, a wealthy man in his own right, was born in India in 1917, the son of a civil engineer and grandson of Wilfrid Ash, of Gilbert-Ash which was a subsidiary of Bovis. He had been a friend of Young since they met when studying at London University and Young had introduced him to Dartington. There he met, and in 1947 married, the Elmhirsts' daughter Ruth. The couple started farming in Essex and then moved to Sharpham House, an eighteenth-century Palladian mansion on a large estate alongside the River Dart. Ash, deeply influenced by the Austrian philosopher Ludwig Wittgenstein and interested in the postwar plans for new towns, was chairman of the Town & Country Planning Association and later chairman of the Green Alliance, the all-party environmental lobby group.

To bring much needed business expertise to Dartington, Christopher Zealley was appointed its Director in 1970. He had been with Imperial Chemical Industries and, while working for the Industrial Reorganisation Corporation under the Harold Wilson government, met Young and George Warburg, who was the trust's banking adviser. He later became chairman of the Consumers' Association. 'Making money through companies owned by the trust was hugely tax efficient – far better than having dividends from quoted portfolios,' Zealley commented. 'The entire positive cash flow from those companies went straight to the trustees and they decided how much to invest back into those companies.'

During the early 1970s, however, several of Dartington's many enterprises found themselves in difficulties, exacerbated by the recession triggered by the quadruple rise in oil prices. The recession was having a dire impact, in particular, upon the seriously undercapitalised Staverton Contractors. The trustees were warned by its auditor, David Parkes, senior partner of the accountancy firm Thomson McLintock in Bristol, that the building firm was faced with bankruptcy. 'It was David Parkes who told me things were wrong at Staverton,' Zealley recalled. 'I was getting really worried – I thought we'd have to put Staverton into liquidation and the trustees would feel obliged to pay the creditors. Maurice Ash introduced us to the managing director of Gilbert-Ash, a part of the Bovis Group, in the hope that they would take Staverton off our hands. He said he needed a company like Staverton like a hole in the head.'

A crucial meeting

David Johnstone, later to be a non-executive director of JT Group but then a senior partner of Thomson McLintock which audited JT, then telephoned Christopher. 'David said would I like to meet this man John Pontin who might be able to help Staverton,' Christopher said. 'I knew nothing about JT and John knew nothing about Dartington. Staverton was operating in his territory but Staverton was mainly a public works contractor and his business was design and build. John came to Dartington and we had lunch with Maurice and Michael Young – a jolly lunch – John talked about the problems with the progressive school called Durdham Park which he had started in Bristol.'

David Perry had bought the Durdhamside sites in Bristol and three had been developed as flats; however, one house, Durdham Park owned by Millgrange, remained undeveloped. John had had the idea of setting up a school and agreed to buy the house for that purpose. 'John was rather different from us – a young chap with engaging qualities but a tough nut underneath it all,' Christopher commented. 'He was clearly very taken with the visionary aspect of Dartington and the way things were discussed there, as though there were no limits in this world to what might be achieved. One might even say he was bewitched by Dartington. We said we would introduce him to our school people and they would see if they could help with Durdham Park – not as a contract but an understanding.' (Durdham Park was later considered to be unviable and was closed within a few years)

At the legal completion meeting, when John was arranging to acquire Staverton Contractors, Maurice Ash humorously remarked, 'I have never felt so happy about something of which I have understood so little.' Christopher said: 'We got to know and like John and we started to work things out about how to deal with Staverton. John said the deal would have to be realistic in fairness to his other shareholders. However, he said, he would be prepared to offer, quite separately from the deal, a gift to the trust of 10 per cent of his company out of his personal holding. We later agreed that this 10 per cent of JT Group should go into a separate trust, the Pontin Charitable Trust, whose initial trustees were the same as Dartington's. The deal was done and Dartington got far more out of it than I ever expected.'

Staverton Contractors became wholly owned by JT while Dartington took an 18 per cent shareholding in the group and thereafter received dividends. Christopher Zealley, who had become managing trustee of Dartington, joined the JT board in 1976 to represent Dartington Hall and remains a group director. In the late 1970s, Christopher and David Johnstone set up Dartington & Co, a merchant bank based in Bristol and owned by the trust to assist small businesses in the rural South-west.

Turbulent time

By the end of the decade, the trustees recognised that, with its multifarious enterprises, Dartington was paying a price for growth. 'It is now a large organisation in danger of becoming fragmented,' stated a published report. 'The many different parts, encouraged to operate independently, have become isolated from each other…Dartington, with all its imperfections, still offers the hope of a sane alternative to the social and spiritual disintegration of modern urban life.'

Dartington Hall School itself was foundering for many reasons. In its early days, the pupils came from middle-class families and their parents had been brought up conventionally and in formal education. The Dartington parents believed progressive schools to be a much better idea. But from the 1960s onwards, parental attitudes generally had greatly relaxed. In Christopher's opinion, 'Home life had become liberal and easy going, certainly undisciplined in any formal sense. Consequently children coming to Dartington actually needed a more, rather than a less, structured framework since they had little in their home lives. The school's ethos simply did not provide that structure.' Drug-taking and sexual liberation during the 'hippie generation' was difficult enough to control in traditional schools and well-nigh impossible in a school like Dartington.

John Wightwick, who had been its head for 10 years, retired in 1983, stating that 'it is a place that matters, for all its faults.' He was succeeded by Lyn Blackshaw who, while working in the US as a director of an educational consultancy, had applied for the post. His wife Beth attracted particular attention, and was described by the school magazine as 'the most talked about woman at Dartington,' wearing an 'eye-catching wardrobe.' The magazine quoted her as saying: 'This is not a typical school, therefore I will not be a typical headmaster's wife.'

The headship certainly proved untypical. Her husband, when he suspected pupils were taking drugs, summoned police to search the premises. The predictable publicity in the national press, including pictures of the Blackshaws, led to unexpected consequences. A photographer recognised Beth as a woman he had filmed some years previously for a provocative centre-page spread in a men's magazine. He recalled that he had also taken photographs of both of them for a pornographic magazine published at about the same time. After further newspaper revelations, the trust decided Blackshaw must resign and, eventually, he quit. While seeking to recover from the affair, the school took another blow when a girl pupil, an heiress of the family who owned the Clarks shoe company in Somerset, was found drowned in the river Dart. Only a year later there was a second tragedy. A young boy pupil accidentally drove a motorbike through a glass door and killed himself. A member of staff who witnessed it had a nervous breakdown and the teaching staff became even more demoralised.

At this turbulent time, Ash stood down as chairman. Writing in January 1984, in a presumably despondent mood and feeling his efforts over the years had been largely wasted, he said that Dartington 'will be well if it listens to itself: that is, if it stays true to its poetry. For Dartington was conceived of poetry, not rational thought. It was not for nothing that Leonard Elmhirst spoke of his mentor, Tagore, simply as The Poet... Dartington should likewise be warned to listen to its own poetry, and take it as its guide.'

10 Dartington's change of chair
John Pontin heads it for 13 years

Dartington Hall has been the focus of an extraordinary range of activities and initiatives. Dartington Plus website, 2004

After Maurice Ash stood down as chairman of Dartington Hall in 1984, the trustees decided he should be succeeded by John Pontin, who had been made a trustee four years earlier. He was valued for his broad and practical business experience and his fascination with the potential for Dartington. Michael Young, who had accepted a life peerage in 1978 as Lord Young of Dartington, was again not chosen but was deputy chairman. John himself admitted he was at first 'full of doubt' when asked to be chairman. 'Dartington at the time seemed a daunting prospect,' he stated. 'I remember being deeply touched by the many expressions of warmth and goodwill following my appointment which bolstered me enormously.'

Ash and his wife Ruth stayed as trustees and, after her death, he set up a college during 1984 at their Sharpham House for Buddhist studies to promote spiritual education. Their farm was converted to the bio-dynamic principles of self-sustaining organic farming initiated by the Austrian philosopher and scientist Rudolf Steiner. Other trustees were Eric Dancer, who headed Dartington businesses including Dartington Glass; John Lane, chairman of Beaford Centre; Prue Quicke, an artist and farmer who initiated the concept of share-farming on the estate, replacing the earlier management model; and Christopher Zealley, chairman of the Consumers' Association (now named Which?) and the Public Interest Research Centre. At that time, in the year to March 1984, Dartington's net worth was £19.75m – almost half of the valuation being its land and buildings – but its income deficit was £115,000. 'We must embrace change if we are to thrive,' John Pontin wrote in his first report, 'but I like to think that links with the past can be maintained and valued.'

Dartington Hall School, however, was reeling from its troubles. With nowhere near a full complement of pupils, it had an annual deficit of £156,000. John reported that 'the school has lived through one of the most difficult periods in its history.' Changes, he wrote, were 'both needed and welcome.' The trustees merged its Aller Park Middle School with Foxhole Senior School in 1985. That summer, the school marked its 60th anniversary on its Foundation Day with its magazine reporting: 'The trustees, now under the chairmanship of John Pontin, by their commitment to the planning of the day and the day itself, showed their continued concern with Dartington employees and residents. The afternoon was an opportunity for us all to enjoy the beautiful setting of the Hall and gardens and to meet our friends. In addition, there were fascinating displays of Dartington and Wedgwood glass, Honnor Marine boats, and Staverton furniture in the Great Hall. On the lawns, among the sideshows, was a stall showing some beautiful jewellery made by students at the school.'

The trustees, who recognised that the school had been an antidote to conventional schools which had repressive regimes, had to decide whether to carry on financing it or to close it at a year's notice – which itself would be costly. Despite objections and pleas by many parents, staff and pupils, the school was closed in 1987. Richard Boston, whose magazine *The Vole* was backed by Dartington, wrote later in *The Guardian* that the school 'was considered, according to taste, progressive and enlightened or shocking and depraved …The once-great school went haywire, filling tabloid front pages before tragi-comically self-destructing.'

Credibility needed

After the school's much-publicised collapse and closure, Dartington's commercial enterprises needed to maintain credibility with banks and businesses. 'We have to ask ourselves regularly if we can afford to spread resources more widely or whether our first duty should be to our well-established home base and, of course, there is no simple answer,' John stated. 'But it is my conviction that Dartington has a spirit – a way of working and a sense of partnership – that has a wide applicability. I hope that over the years our outposts will grow, flourish and nurture us all.'

He took the view, though, that Dartington was too ramified by all its activities. The trustees, having only superficial knowledge of every individual enterprise, were faced with an unworkable burden. Christopher commented: 'The proliferation of initiatives bogged the trustees down in a fog of incomprehension, varying between blissful happiness that it was all happening, and utter misery when things went wrong, and a sense of being responsible but without any actual effectiveness in their role.'

After the acquisition of Staverton Contractors, but before John had become a trustee, a joint enterprise had been set up between Dartington and JT. 'The trust was short of ready money,' Christopher recalled. 'Both the trust and JT had a lot of non-essential property which it was not timely to put on the market, so we had formed a joint company to borrow against those assets – we called this company Tiltyard. The new company was owned equally by the trust and JT and they each sold properties into it, independently valued.' By this means, cash was released to the two shareholders. They both benefited from being able to sell surplus property assets at the most advantageous time, rather than when they were in a hurry for cash.

The trustees and JT's board approved the Tiltyard scheme but, at some point, Young apparently became suspicious that Tiltyard was somehow benefiting JT Group rather than Dartington. Probably prompted by his questioning, the Charity Commission launched an investigation into the trust's affairs including the valuation of the Tiltyard properties. Its interminable inquiry ran for seven years until the commissioners eventually closed the matter, neither exonerating any of the parties nor pressing any charges, having found no evidence of misconduct.

The commission's inquiry did lasting damage to Dartington. Its ponderous procedures exacerbated personal differences between the trustees and soured what was otherwise a successful period of restructuring the programmes and enterprises. The organisation needed to be less fragmented and more professionally managed. While Dartington never wished to be regarded as a conventional institution, it had little alternative but to present itself as such.

Staverton sold

One profitable business was Dartington Glass, in which £40,000 had been originally invested to set up the business. Annual turnover had reached £6m and the trustees saw the merit of divesting the business at a handsome return. Complex but profitable deals were struck, first with the sale to the Wedgwood Group of a 51 per cent stake and then a buy-back, and finally a stepped sale to Rockware Glass based on a £7m valuation.

JT Group, meanwhile, had always hoped to make the Staverton building company a design and build subsidiary. Overall, Staverton made reasonable profits on low margins although it suffered from a shortage of contracts during the industry's cyclical downturns. But its management remained unconverted to a fully-fledged design and build operation. This led to JT's decision to dispose of the company, stating that the reason for selling it 'underlines the group's specialisation in the design and build approach to construction.' It was sold in May 1990 to a construction and property company, Farr Group, of Westbury in Wiltshire, for an immediate cash offer of £1.6m with a further deferred payment of £890,000. Farr Group itself became insolvent seven months later and did not make the deferred payment. Fortunately, the Staverton members of the group pension scheme had not been transferred to the Farr scheme and, although jobs were lost, pension rights survived.

Dartington, however, retained its JT shareholding. Dartington & Co, the merchant bank, had expanded its capital base and eventually came under the control of John Hemingway and his associates. In 1991, as the national economy downturned, property values suffered and it was decided to put Dartington & Co into voluntary liquidation. The banking department was closed, depositors repaid and the loan book recovered over a period. The stockbroking and corporate finance activities were spun off as Rowan Dartington in a management buy-out.

Rationalising their responsibilities, the trustees set about disposing of other satellite enterprises such as the Beaford Centre and North Devon Trust (which supports environmental projects) and Morwellham Quay, a visitor attraction in the Tamar Valley. These became independent charities with Dartington transferring a modest part of its endowment to each of them. The trust, after the closure of Dartington Hall School, had to reaffirm its commitment to education as one of its key charitable objectives. Park School, a small fee-paying primary, was set up on the estate by a group of parents and teachers but independent of the trust. It was conceived as a progressive model to emphasise environmental issues, visual arts and music. John Pontin and his fellow trustees decided that there should also be a college.

Schumacher College

The college would be based on the theories of Dr E.F. Schumacher, the economist and philosopher. Schumacher, best known as the author of *Small is Beautiful* (1973, republished in 1999 by Hartley & Marks) had died in 1977 and Schumacher UK was founded as a society the following year, with its first meeting held in Bristol and attended by Maurice Ash and John Pontin. Ash and fellow trustee John Lane were among contributors to the magazine *Resurgence* which published articles 'on the cutting edge of current thinking, promoting creativity, ecology, spirituality and frugality.' It has been edited since the 1970s by Satish Kumar who, born in India and a former Jain monk, founded in 1982 the pioneering Small School in Hartland, Devon, with ecological and spiritual values.

These connections caused the trustees to launch the residential college as 'an international centre for ecological studies.' Named Schumacher College, it was established in the Old Postern building at Dartington in 1991. Anne Phillips was a co-founder and became its director, while Satish Kumar became the programme director. The Dalai Lama, its patron, stated: 'The college is founded upon the conviction that a new vision, inspired by concern with what is sacred in nature and human nature, is needed to sustain the Earth.'

Its initial course was by James Lovelock, the scientist and originator of the Gaia theory which – named after the Greek goddess of the Earth – believes that the Earth functions as a living organism, forming a complex system with the capacity to keep the planet fit for life. Short courses followed on the ecological issues of how economic growth causes climate change, deforestation and land degradation, while the majority of the world's population are left in poverty. The college also offers a course on how to make businesses more ecologically sustainable, while an MSc programme is run in collaboration with Plymouth University.

The college receives financial support from the trust as well as from fees and fund raising, while its participants, aged from 18 to 80, have come from 75 countries. Teachers have included Fritjof Capra, author of the *Tao of Physics and Web of Life*; Paul Hawken, author of *The Ecology of Commerce and Natural Capitalism*; Vandana Shiva, the eco-feminist; Rupert Sheldrake, author of *The Rebirth of Nature*; and Jonathon Porritt, chair of the UK Sustainable Development Commission and programme director of Forum for the Future. 'Concern for environment and sustainability underpins all courses,' said Satish Kumar. 'Education which does not address the environmental issues of our time is no education at all.'

Trustees' reshuffle

Christopher Zealley retired in 1988 as the managing trustee but stayed as chairman of the College of Arts and the International Summer School, which had been renamed with dance and music-theatre added. William Glock, who had been the Summer School's artistic director until 1979, had been succeeded until 1984 by Peter Maxwell Davies, many of whose works were premièred there, and then by Gavin Henderson.

In 1997, John Pontin stood down as chairman and was conferred an honorary Master of Arts by Dartington College of Arts in recognition of his services. His connection with Schumacher College continues – he is vice-president of Schumacher UK whose president is Satish Kumar. Ivor Stolliday, the trust's secretary for 11 years until January 2004 and director of JT since October 1998, chairs the Schumacher College Foundation which supports the college's activities.

John Lane, whose books include *Timeless Simplicity – Creative Living in a Consumer Society*, followed John as the trust's chairman. He was succeeded by John van Praag, Kate Caddy (daughter of Maurice and Ruth Ash) and, in 2002, by James Cornford, who has had long personal connections with Dartington and the Elmhirst family. Much of his career, after a professorship at Edinburgh University, was with the Nuffield and Paul Hamlyn Foundations. He was involved in setting up the School for Social Entrepreneurs, founded in 1997 by Lord Young, and co-chairs the Campaign for Freedom of Information. 'The Elmhirsts left us a marvellous legacy, but we cannot be like them,' James said in a lecture in 2003. 'If there is to be renewal or reinvigoration at Dartington, it will have to be by other means than their inspired patronage. We will certainly not succeed by standing still or attempting to put the clock back.'

Today, Dartington's remaining businesses continue on sustainable development principles. Dartington Hall Farms manages the agricultural estate and Dartington Trading Co. runs the Cider Press Centre and Totnes Bookshop (Ken Stradling, a former deputy chairman of Dartington Trading Co and managing director of Bristol Guild, was meanwhile appointed a trustee of Arnolfini) The Cider Press Centre, in the converted farm buildings, has 11 shops, two restaurants, a plant centre and woodturning workshop. It attracts 600,000 visitors a year and holds regular craft exhibitions. Other businesses are Dartington Accommodation & Catering Services – there are courtyard bedrooms and conference rooms – and Dartington Property Corporation, which manages land and property. The trust, in addition to its shareholding in JT Group which had risen through share buy-backs to 20 per cent, has a 26 per cent stake in Grant Instruments. The company designs and makes laboratory equipment at the village Shepreth near Cambridge, endorsing the Elmhirsts' desire to encourage rural employment.

John Pontin, with Kate Caddy, trustee, and sculptor Peter Randall-Page at the unveiling of *Jacob's Pillow* at Dartington Hall in May, 2005. The sculpture was commissioned by John to mark a 30-year relationship with Dartington.

While all these activities have followed from the Elmhirsts' ideas, the amount of income generated is inadequate to enable the trustees to pursue a continuing programme of innovative projects. The difficulty relates back to the understanding that, during Dorothy Elmhirst's lifetime, the trust could receive extra money from her when necessary. That era is in the past and the trust needs support from all the sources available, both public and private. Direct subsidies are still given to activities which include the Summer School, Dartington Arts (which runs a year-round programme of music, theatre, dance and film) and Schumacher College, although fees and grants from other bodies carry the main burden. Funding is also required for the gardens and woodlands, craft education, the archive and collection at High Cross House, and the care of the buildings.

The personal links with the Elmhirsts are now less than they were. Ruth Ash, daughter of the Elmhirsts, died in 1986, Lord Young in 2002 and Maurice Ash in 2003. *The Times* obituary (February 6 2003) described Ash as a 'fervent supporter of civic, artistic and environmental causes' and stated that his 'overriding fear was of rampant but fragile egotism undermining civilisation.' Christopher Zealley and Ivor Stolliday, who previously had been company secretary and personnel director of Television South West, remain on JT's board. Ivor, after retiring as the trust's secretary, has taken on the role of developing a residential fellowship programme at Dartington for creative people, with the activities ranging from sculpture to ecology and from choreography to philosophy.

Cultural flagship

Dartington, despite its preoccupation with finance and lacking core funding from government, is still a cultural flagship. It describes itself on its website as 'a continuing experiment in the relationship of the arts to education, community, economy, the environment and well-being.' In March 2003, Arts Council England (it had been formed as a single national organisation in 2002) awarded a £1m grant over three years for the new Dartington Plus initiative. As a centre of excellence in music, Dartington Plus is a partnership embracing Dartington Arts, the International Summer School, College of Arts and King Edward VI Community College in Totnes. The annual review of 2003-04 stated that the trust and subsidiary companies had incoming resources of £10.2m and commitments of £11.3m. Ivor, reporting on the annual review in March 2004, wrote that the year 'was one of great change that saw continued development and success for the charitable programmes at Dartington, and renewed impetus in dealing with the challenges faced by the trust as a whole.' Vaughan Lindsay was appointed as chief executive officer after Ivor's retirement.

The College of Arts, associated since 1990 with Plymouth University which validates its degrees, is one of only four UK institutions for performance arts. Schumacher College, while seeking to raise £5m to renovate its Old Postern building, plans closer links with Plymouth University. Its short courses have more than 250 students from many countries and a popular series of evening lectures. The International Summer School is, as ever, an annual highpoint, together with the 'Ways With Words' literary festival. As Charlotte Higgins, writing in *The Guardian* (April 2003) described Dartington, 'It is Janus-faced: inward and outward-looking, local and international, medieval and modernist.' The 'Ways With Words' website stated: 'For those who love gardens, beautiful buildings, books and ideas, it's a perfect place to be.'

JT's long-term connection with Dartington continues and, in many ways, it still keeps a more personal relationship than Dartington's shareholding in the company. 'Thanks to a very generous gift from John Pontin,' the trust said, it was able to commission Peter Randall-Page to create a sculpture. Named *Jacob's Pillow*, of Jacob's stone pillow in *Genesis*, it was the first new sculpture to be commissioned for the gardens since the 1940s. It was unveiled in May 2005. 'I shall never forget the moment when the cover came off Jacob's Pillow and we were all spellbound with its beauty,' John said. Reflecting that day upon his long association with Dartington, he remarked: 'Dartington became my university.'

11 Peaks and troughs
JT Design Build's final years

It was the best of times, it was the worst of times.
Charles Dickens (*A Tale of Two Cities*, 1859)

Britain's economy was transformed during the 1980s when Margaret Thatcher was a dominant prime minister with the Conservatives in government throughout the decade. Thatcher intended the economy to be much more competitive with freer markets and less trade union power. Service industries gained as old-style manufacturing fell into decline. Construction continued to be a fragmented and combative industry and with its differing social classes. Changes in design and specification, alterations in the client's requirements, modifications during construction and inflation resulted in huge cost overruns on mega-projects. Those included the Thames Barrier, originally estimated at £23m and which cost twice the amount; Barbican Arts Centre, with an initial estimate of £17m but which came to £80m; NatWest Tower, estimated at £15m and which cost £115m; and Humber Bridge, with an estimate of £19m and which reached £120m.

Throughout the country, retail development responded to the rampant consumer demand. 'The spectre of revolution is once again haunting Britain. Now it is the retail revolution that could leave many towns and cities as shattered as if a political revolution had occurred,' *The Guardian* wrote (September 16, 1987), commenting on the superstores and out-of-town retail warehouses, 'The real tragedy is that where once cities and towns were places for all kinds of activities…the retail revolution has given them one overriding purpose: shopping.'

By the end of the 1980s, the national boom in construction led to there being no fewer than 200,000 building firms, three times as many as in 1970. The industry's structure had changed – principally owing to the shift towards small firms of sub-contractors and the huge number of one-man businesses. Since 1970, when some 210 companies each employed over 600 staff, firms of that size had reduced to about 100 and many had become subsidiaries of conglomerates. Leading contractors by 1990, ranked by turnover, were:

BICC	Tarmac (now Carillion)
Trafalgar House	AMEC
Wimpey	Bovis
John Laing	Mowlem
Costain	Taylor Woodrow

As ever, the demand for construction was not matched by the availability of skills. According to *The Construction Industry of Great Britain* (Roger C. Harvey and Allan Ashworth, Butterworth-Heinemann 1993), the industry at the end of the 1980s needed to recruit over 80,000 people annually just to replace employment wastage. 'Unfortunately, not only has construction an image of a difficult, demanding and unbecoming occupation with an adversarial culture, but it is not seen as progressive, offering further training or financial advantages…Schools are not well informed about the construction industry. It is seen to be male-dominated and, particularly at the craft level, unattractive to women and ethnic minorities.'

Peak turnover

At the turn of the decade, there was further political turmoil. The demolition of the Berlin Wall in 1989 led to the disintegration of the Soviet Union. The Conservative government was in disarray when Nigel Lawson resigned as Chancellor that autumn because of his disagreements with Thatcher, and in 1990, there were violent street protests against the government's revised rating system, called a community charge but condemned as a 'poll tax'. In October of that year, the government joined the European Exchange Rate Mechanism (ERM), which was soon to prove a disastrous decision for the economy. Geoffrey Howe, the long-serving minister, resigned in protest at Thatcher's combative attitude to the European Community, his resignation speech leading to Thatcher's downfall that November after 11 years at Downing Street. John Major succeeded her as PM.

JT Group's turnover peaked in 1988-89 at £55m with pre-tax profits of £3.06m – JT's previous pre-tax profits had reached close to £5m. Peter Burchill joined the company that year as the group's chief executive. Almost all the office space at Bush House was used by JT and its business partners, with the design and build project teams remaining on the top floor. A new venture, The Bush Consultancy, was set up in 1989 with Bob Hunt heading it, providing site procurement and design services to the country club, hotel and leisure industry. It formed a joint venture, PGA Golf Management, with the Professional Golfers' Association in 1992. This was led by Barry Pipkin and Norman McIndoe, who had been with Country Club Hotels, and focused on providing management and marketing solutions for golf course developers and owners. Its first contract was with Oaklands Golf & Country Club in Cheshire. The Bush Consultancy also used the modular system which JT Design Build had installed as bedroom units at Redwood Lodge, The Grange and South Marston Country Club, Swindon.

Nationally, the boom in construction was ending and Staverton Contractors had been sold in May 1990. The economy had grown too fast and rising inflation led to a deep recession in the early 1990s. Joint ventures were often a preferred approach within the property market but Sheraton-JT also became a victim of the slump in the market. JT sold to Sheraton's parent company, Sheraton Securities International (SSI), its own interests in 36 acres north of Bristol, known as Bristol Business Park – later developed as the massive headquarters of the Ministry of Defence Procurement Executive. SSI, however, was in financial difficulties. In August 1990, JT agreed to support a rescue plan at a cost of £2.5m. This was substantially to protect the £17m project of a 200-bed Holiday Inn in Cambridge which was being undertaken by Sheraton-JT and of which JT Design Build was the contractor.

The hotel was completed but the rescue plan failed to save SSI. The joint venture was wound up and, in April 1991, receivers were appointed for SSI. The Royal Fine Art Commission issued a contentious publication called *What Makes A Good Building?* in 1994 which criticised design and build, denigrating in particular the Cambridge Holiday Inn. The façade's design, however, had not been determined by JT but by Holiday Inn. The commission's publication did not credit JT's completion on time and within budget, while the client was said to have been delighted with the project. Structurally, this had been JT's most ambitious project as the brief required parking for 350 cars on three floors under the six-storey hotel. The site was surrounded by important and vibration-sensitive buildings including university laboratories. The rarely used 'top down' system of construction was deployed by engineer Mike Boyce. This allowed the underground floors to be built at the same time as the above ground structure.

Recession bites

In December 1990, JT reported: 'Against the background of one of the worst recessions on record to affect companies in the construction and property sectors, our core business JT Design Build has performed well with profits up 53 per cent although on a slightly reduced turnover.' The next month, the Gulf War began after Saddam Hussein had ordered the Iraqi army to invade its small neighbour Kuwait. A United Nations' 28-member military coalition, including the UK and under US command, achieved the liberation of Kuwait in late February, while Saddam Hussein remained in power with ominous consequences.

By the year ending December 1991, JT Design Build's turnover was £32.8m with a trading profit of £3.02m. Its average number of employees was 151, down by 31 since the previous year. 'Once again,' its report stated, 'the company has performed well in a very difficult trading period. Turnover was down considerably, as forecast last year, but profitability was well maintained as a result of profitable contracts secured in 1990.' Among that year's projects were the refurbishment and extension of Bristol City Football Club, a fire station at Stansted airport and Jubilee House at Gatwick. The company had been particularly successful in winning airport contracts, having previously built Cardinal Point, a five-storey office at Heathrow. JT Design Build reported that Jubilee House, a £10.5m five-storey office development won on open tender, 'was completed in 13 months, just over two months early.' Martin Peach, BAA's project manager, stated: 'We set JT a tight deadline to undertake and complete the Jubilee House project. JT not only got inside our deadline but managed to slice two months off the time set, while attaining the highest quality standards.' He added that he had been impressed by the 'tremendous enthusiasm and spirit of co-operation of the JT team. There was absolutely no friction on the site.'

Many other sizeable projects in the early 1990s included £720,000 student accommodation for Bristol University with modular bedroom units, a £3.6m newspaper headquarters and printing plant at Exeter, an £18m 170-bedroomed leisure hotel for Boddingtons in Blackpool, and the £5m Chilworth Manor Conference Centre for South-ampton University. That centre's project concluded many years of master planning and development of its large science park. The contract involved repair and alterations to the listed manor and extensions to provide 60 hotel bedrooms as well as the conference hall and health club with all furniture, fitting and equipment. JT's involvement in Country Club Hotels provided valuable know-how for the university's new scheme.

The conversion of Chilworth Manor and the historic Breadsall Priory into a £10m country club hotel were both commended. 'Accepted wisdom has it that design and build is suited to basic building types, rather than to restoring historic buildings, which call for sensitivity, ingenuity and patience,' wrote Martin Spring, an editor of *Building* magazine. 'This neat theory, however, is overturned by two prestigious restoration schemes of historic country houses painstakingly carried out by JT Design Build on fast-track contracts...In both schemes, modern facilities and building services were imperceptibly infiltrated into the historic structures. Ornate plaster cornices, ceilings and mouldings, for instance, were preserved by hiding pipes and ducts in disused chimney stacks, chases through thick brick walls, and floor depths. Original French-polished hardwood doors and panelling were also retained, thanks to a complex fire-prevention package.'

Management changes

Des Williams, who had been a highly regarded manager at JT since he joined in 1965, died of a heart attack in February 1991. He had been managing director of JT Design Build until his move to Arabuild in 1975. Since his return from Dubai, he had been a valued group board member. John Pontin described him as 'a great friend and colleague whose skills and unstinting efforts helped make JT what it is today.'

He had been chairman of Bristol City Football Club and helped to revive the club after it slumped deep into debt. It had been relegated from Division One in 1980, relegated the

John Pontin on Narrow Quay, Bristol with Watershed in the background.

John Pontin with colleagues, 2005. *Left to right*: John Pontin, Ivor Stolliday, Ben Pontin (John's son), Tim Miles, Christopher Zealley and David Johnstone.

Bush House.

JT Design Build project team at work, Bush House.

Offices for Ashfield District Council, Derbyshire.

Goodwood Golf & Country Club: a Country Club Hotels development.

Waterlooville Swimming Pool, Havant.

Detail, services installation,
Clevedon Swimming Pool.

Municipality Building, Dubai, built by Arabuild Ltd.

Reinforcement for 350-space underground car park for Holiday Inn, Cambridge.

Bristol Business Park: the first building on this 100-acre business park near Parkway Station.

Courtyard, Bristol Business Park.

Enterprise House: Stansted Airport, for BAA plc.

Bristol City Football Club, refurbishment and extension of the existing grandstand.

Jacob's Pillow, sculpture by Peter Randall Page at Dartington Hall, 2005.

70 Prince Street, Bristol. Restoration of listed building, now JT Group offices.

Chew Magna Mill, focal point for the village's Zero Waste project, awaiting sensitive refurbishment (*see* Chapter 14).

next season and yet again the following season. The club recalled that it had 'plunged into financial crisis' in 1982. It was re-formed that year as a new limited company, 'avoiding closure by a whisker.' Des, himself having been a footballer and cricketer, was appointed its chairman and JT provided financial support of £37,500 as the club restructured. The *Western Daily Press* said he had 'worked out a minor financial miracle, pulling away from the depths of the fourth division in the process.' Paying tribute to him after his death, the club's vice-chairman Leslie Kew said: 'He was the quiet man in the background but he has always had his finger on the pulse and he ensured that the financial stability of the club will remain…He never sought the limelight but at the same time he was a man any football club would be proud of.' The then manager, Jimmy Lumsden, said he was 'one of the most honest men I ever met.'

Hunting Aviation, Southampton Airport.

Howard Williams, the brother of Des and managing director of JT Design Build since 1975, retired in 1990 and was succeeded by Richard Demery. Roger Mortimer, deputy chairman of JT Group, retired at the end of 1991. Howard and Roger had reached the long-agreed retirement age of 60. John thanked them for having made 'fundamental contributions to the development and direction of both JT Design Build and the group as a whole.'

Leigh Court bought

During 1992, the board saw an opportunity to acquire a prestigious but dilapidated headquarters at a bargain price: Leigh Court, a mansion in 25 acres of parkland at Abbots Leigh, on the western outskirts of Bristol. The Grade II* mansion was designed in 1814 by Thomas Hooper for a shipowner and banker called Philip Miles and with the grounds landscaped by Humphrey Repton. It was built of Bath stone in the Palladian style, with the interior of Greek Revival. Nikolaus Pevsner, the architectural historian, described it as 'the best house of its date in Somerset, especially excellent inside. Noble Grecian block, with detached pedimented portico of four giant unfluted Ionic columns… The whole composition is worthy of a palace.'

The mansion once had a remarkable collection of works by old masters, including paintings by Poussin, Raphael, Rubens and Titian, but these were sold by the Miles family

Leigh Court, Bristol.

who later sold the house in 1915. It became an institution for 'persons requiring care and protection' managed by the National Health Service as a hospital from 1957 until 1985. After a short period as a home to St. Christopher's School, it was sold in 1988 to a private company which had intended to convert it to office use. Instead, it went into receivership and JT bought the mansion and estate in 1992 for just over £500,000.

JT started to restore the house to its former splendour and at considerable expense; its roof needed complete renovation. In co-operation with English Heritage, offices were to be made on the second floor. The construction industry, however, was then in a downturn during the national recession and so the board decided to retain its base in Bush House. Together with Leigh Court Associates, JT reopened the mansion for conferences and functions and with serviced office accommodation. It let the mansion to commercial tenants and Bristol Chamber of Commerce & Initiative. On the Leigh Court estate, John Pontin, in partnership with James Bruges and Marion Wells, revived the historic walled garden through their charitable trusts and introduced educational courses on organic horticulture. Organic produce was grown in the two-acre garden and sold at Bristol's weekly Farmers Market, to local companies and through a box scheme to local residents.

Design Build suffers

New contracts were ever scarcer as the recession bit deeper in the early 1990s, with property prices collapsing by as much as 50 per cent in some parts of the country. Nevertheless, the Tories, led by John Major, won a fourth consecutive victory in the April 1992 general election. Interest base rates soared to defend sterling but, by September, the government was forced to devalue sterling and quit the ERM. The following year, the Maastricht Treaty was ratified to enable a closer economic and political union in Europe.

JT Design Build's turnover had slumped by a third to £21.6m in 1992, with its tight margins causing the group as a whole to make a loss of £586,000. Forecasts of continuing losses caused JT to exercise its option to sell its remaining 25 per cent interest in Country Club Hotels to Whitbread for £14.7m. This produced a one-off profit of £2.9m, enabling JT to repay bank borrowings and therefore eliminating interest charges. But JT Design Build was still 'severely affected' by the lack of orders and over-capacity in 1993, the chairman stated. 'The company experienced a small drop in turnover to £19.3m which, when combined with the low margins available, contributed significantly to our overall loss for the year.'

The board now decided that, with the current market restricted and margins under severe pressure, there needed to be a change in the way the company operated. Unexpectedly, JT's board was contacted 'out of the blue' by Roy Paramor, who had design and build experience with Condor but which had ceased trading. He said he had the funds to buy a company and asked if JT would sell its design and build business. Paramor – who was described as 'ebullient' – indicated that he could source the funds to acquire the whole of JT Design Build. It subsequently transpired that he could not. The board then agreed to allow him and his associates to acquire 25 per cent of the company with JT Group retaining the balance of 75 per cent, and with Paramor leading a management buy-in team.

'Roy and his team have considerable experience in the design and build field,' John Pontin stated, 'and their particular skills will enable JT Design Build to enter hitherto unexplored and closed markets and to develop further the company's reputation as a high quality provider of building services.' Paramor himself declared: 'We looked at over 40 companies before identifying JT for the management buy-in. We were attracted by the company's remarkable reputation for quality buildings across the broad spectrum of industrial and commercial work.' He claimed that the design and build companies now accounted for about 40 per cent of all construction. 'By the end of the century this is expected to have increased to 60-70 per cent.'

Two investment properties were sold for a total of £851,000 while JT retained a half-share of land at Ashton Vale, on the outskirts of south-west Bristol, that it had acquired in 1991 from Newcombe Estates, who retained the other 50% interest. This joint venture resulted from an earlier relationship when JT had built 24 houses for the Newcombes at Portbury – 25 years before! In 1994, JT Design Build was awarded the building contract at Ashton Vale, with the combined deal worth about £6m, for the creation of a David Lloyd Leisure tennis centre and a park-and-ride facility for commuters and shoppers. Roy Paramor, however, changed JT Design Build's organisation. 'Although we will remain a dedicated design and build contractor,' he stated, 'the design element will no longer be exclusively in-house.' This altered the original concept of design and build. JT now had to be more in common with construction companies which promoted the commercial advantages of design and build but adopted a less defined approach.

End of an era

JT Group needed to reduce the group's substantial bank borrowings and to improve its liquidity. The board decided to place the freehold of Bush House on the market but without quitting the property. 'We received an offer of £5.4m for our freehold interest which we found very satisfactory,' the chairman stated. 'The resulting funds have had an extremely positive impact on the liquidity of the group.' The sale was completed in July 1994 to Ivory Gate (UK), a property investment company based in Gibraltar. JT then leased back part of the building, staying there as its headquarters, and with Arnolfini's 150-year underlease retained at the peppercorn rent of 5p per annum, plus its share of service charges.

That July, Peter Burchill resigned as chief executive. John Pontin, hoping that the British economy was beginning to come out of recession, said: 'The new management team which have been running JT Design Build for a year have made a significant impact on both the marketing of the company's services and its methods of operation.' Paramor, though, then established his own company, Roy Paramor Associates, to provide consultancy advice on design and build and Private Finance Initiatives. (The PFI had been introduced by the Tories for the finance of new buildings in the public sector)

The construction market was still failing to revive. The property development industry and consequently builders were subjected to a recession that had been the most severe in a 60-year cycle. Many large as well as small companies went out of business and nearly a third of the workforces lost their jobs. By the end of 1994, JT Design Build had incurred a substantial loss of £2.1m with the group as a whole incurring a loss of £2.87m. There was a black hole in its order book. 'The board concluded that the future prospects for JT Design Build would be better served by being part of a larger group and approaches were made to several of the larger UK companies,' the chairman reported.

A deal was agreed with the construction company Higgs & Hill, which acquired the business and current contracts of JT Design Build with effect from December 31 1994 and completed on May 2 1995. Some months later, Higgs & Hill merged the Design Build business with its existing operations, although retaining the name. Soon after, at the end of 1996, Higgs & Hill sold its own construction division to Hollandsche Beton Groep, the Dutch international construction company, and changed the name of its remaining business to Swan Hill. JT Design Build had ceased to exist.

12 On the waterfront: City's social and cultural centre

Rebuilding the economy of a dilapidated waterfront district can provide cultural and recreational opportunities, spark commercial and residential development, and preserve history. World Architecture *magazine, June 2000*

JT Group, after the disposal of JT Design Build in May 1995, was a different and smaller organisation, with employees no longer directly involved in site-building work. During the construction market's slump in the early 1990s, the company's workforce had fallen from 250 people to about 120 when it was decided to sell JT Design Build. There were more redundancies as the reorganised group was streamlined to concentrate on property development and investment, with staff numbers soon falling to 50.

The company now focused on Bristol's redundant Floating Harbour. John Pontin, in his annual report, stated: 'There is a very high level of tenant interest in our waterfront properties and I expect redevelopment to commence in 1996…This development has the potential to generate significant rental flows and value for the group in the future.' Other property developers were showing interest after a long hiatus since the 1980s, when the cultural and arts-led activity by Arnolfini at Bush House and Watershed Media Centre had been the only flag-bearers of rejuvenation. In February 1987, an article in *Chartered Surveyor Week*, had judged that the 'whole maritime area represents one of the most attractive development opportunities in the heart of any British city.' The only new build, however, was the retail headquarters of Lloyds Bank, completed in 1990. Lloyds, with its hundreds of staff, had been wooed to Bristol by the city council which offered it a quayside position on the semi-derelict Canon's Marsh.

Although Lloyds' post-modernist white buildings were impressive, the offices themselves would not attract visitors to the waterfront. The bank hoped its headquarters would encourage other development around it, with the fine setting which gave views of Bristol cathedral, St Mary Redcliffe church and the hillside backdrop of Georgian and Victorian terraces. Lloyds' open amphitheatre on the quayside was occasionally used for outdoor concerts, while the bank sponsored an annual regatta in the Floating Harbour. But attempts to regenerate the 66-acre site of Canon's Marsh stalled, mired by the complexities of land ownership, the local politicals and the recession in the property market. The site around Lloyds stayed bleakly vacant, only providing acres of space for car parking.

Arnolfini's revamp

Arnolfini itself, after the resignation of Jeremy Rees and the appointment of Barry Barker as director, revamped its home at Bush House after its funding troubles had led to the closure of jewellery exhibitions and a video library. Barker commissioned the architect David Chipperfield to refurbish the galleries and to collaborate with the artist Bruce McLean to design the café-bar. The café-bar, with fixed wooden benches, opened in 1988 and gained much popularity as the first 'style' bar in the city.

Barker was on the jury next year of the Turner Prize, when the shortlist of remarkable artists included Richard Long, Gillian Ayres, Lucian Freud and Paula Rego. Long, who had been shortlisted in three previous years, was awarded the prize. Born in Bristol in 1945, he studied at the West of England College of Art and then at St. Martin's School of Art, London. His sculptural art, intimately close to landscape, had been shown at Arnolfini. The art critic Richard Cork, wrote in *The Times*, (May 29 2004): 'Long is an intensely private man, a natural loner who has always been based in his native Bristol and pursued a single-minded vision of the world.' He quoted Long as saying: 'I'm a classical artist concentrating on lines, circles and fundamental geometry. But I use lots of different media, and every stone or splash of mud is different. So I think it articulates the cosmic variety of nature.' In 1990, Barker left Arnolfini (since 2001 he has headed the Centre for Contemporary Visual Arts at the University of Brighton) and was succeeded by Tessa Jackson in the following spring. Jackson, who became director for eight years, had been head of the visual arts, architecture and film programme in Glasgow, preparing for when it was designated European City of Culture in 1990.

While Canon's Marsh remained fallow, Bristol as a whole had lost much of its architectural character. A *Times* article, published in May 1990, headlined 'A mercantile city brought down by craze for change.' It stated: 'The beautiful city has been replaced by a concrete jungle of motorways, overpasses, hideous shopping centres and gimcrack office blocks. Bristol is now one of the most ugly, depressing places in Britain.' Although this was overstated – there were many genuinely ugly places in the country – the city engineers had indeed damaged the historic built environment. St Mary Redcliffe church, with its pinnacle spire nearly 300ft high, had been described by Queen Elizabeth I as 'the fairest, goodliest and most famous parish church in England.' It was now crudely marooned by dual-lane highways. Cumberland Basin, linking the Floating Harbour to the river Avon towards Bristol Channel, was spoiled by spaghetti roads of concrete underpasses and overpasses.

The city centre was ever tattier. In 1990, *Bristol Evening Post* ran a series under the title: 'Bristol: what's gone wrong?' As with other cities, there was the 'doughnut' effect common in the US, with the core being hollowed by out-of town business parks, shopping malls and greenfield new housing. Much of the speculative housing was outside Bristol's northern boundaries, where a vast estate called Bradley Stoke was built without vernacular merit nor a village heart. The sudden collapse of house prices, during the early 1990s' recession, caused residents with 'negative equity' mortgages to nickname the place as 'Sadly Broke.'

The Initiative's vision

During the national recession, Bristol was also a city of political conflict. The Conservative government had set up Bristol Development Corporation in 1989 on the grounds that, since the Labour-led city council was ill-disposed to property development, there needed to be an agency with compulsory planning powers and a private-sector perspective. The corporation, whose chief executive was less than diplomatic, was fiercely opposed by both Bristol City Council and Avon County Council. Litigation resulted in the designated area being reduced to 364 hectares, comprising a fragmented industrial zone behind Temple Meads station and Upper Avon Valley, an area of derelict industrial premises with land contamination. Bristol and Avon councils were themselves often in conflict; Avon was disliked by many residents as well as by city councillors.

Bristol Initiative had been set up by a steering group of a dozen businessmen, chaired by Tony Shepherd and including John Pontin, and who were alarmed at the city's downward spiral accelerated by divisiveness. The group, launched in 1990 with support from IBM, British Telecom and other businesses including JT, was determined to revitalise the city by forming a public, private and voluntary partnership as a means to tackle the social and economic difficulties. They wanted a fresh vision for the city and a strategy to achieve it. John Savage, a businessman who had run his own transport company and was then a director of Associated Newspapers' subsidiaries, was recruited to head it. Over 100 people who had the most influence in the city region were soon joining the organisation.

The city council was wary of the Initiative but practical relationships began to be formed. Savage and the council's chief executive, Lucy de Groot, were able to agree on many proposed policies. In 1993, the Initiative merged with what had been a lacklustre Chamber of Commerce, with Savage as chief executive of what was named Bristol Chamber of Commerce & Initiative (BCCI). John Pontin joined the board that year. The Initiative was the chamber's driving force, with most members attending quarterly evening meetings, usually at Leigh Court where BCCI was based. It advocated a variety of schemes – ranging from a rough sleepers' project to its 'Building a Better Bristol' awards for practical achievements and the redevelopment of the postwar, dreary shopping centre called Broadmead. A renaissance of Broadmead has been since planned by the Bristol Alliance, a joint venture with Land Securities Group and Hammerson UK Properties for 'modern, fashionable retailing and with offices, homes and leisure that will attract new tenants and residents.'

City arguments

BCCI had stayed entirely detached from the short-lived Bristol Development Corporation which concentrated on 'flagship' schemes. The corporation built a dual-carriageway spine road from the M32 motorway and which was opposed by the city council. The road cost almost half of the corporation's total expenditure of £112m. The other main schemes were a shopping and cinema complex called Avon Meads, a commercial development named Quay Point and housing intended for first-time buyers. Parliamentary consent was granted to build a weir to control the water level of the Avon's New Cut, the tidal river running in parallel to the Floating Harbour and, much of the day, a dreary muddy ditch. But the weir was abandoned because of the cost. Given the usual long gestation period of property schemes, more than 100 tasks were uncompleted when the corporation was wound up in March 1996. An intended sale of Quay Point to the private sector was not achieved and the site was transferred to English Partnerships, the urban regeneration agency.

While BCCI began to share proposals with the city council, it did not always agree. A case in point was the issue of Filton airfield, north of the city boundary. It had opened as early as 1910 and was the home of British Aerospace (BAe) and Rolls-Royce with a long runway from which Concorde's test flights were made. BAe wanted to convert it to an international passenger airport. The site is near the M4 and M5 motorways and a main railway line to London. BCCI supported the scheme as a vital enhancement for the region's economy. But the council opposed it because it owned the city's modest airport at Lulsgate, which had been originally used by the Royal Air Force. That airport, in the countryside south of Bristol, had no direct links to the motorways, no rail connection and an inadequate road into the city.

Filton, though, was next to the reckless spread of greenfield new housing and many residents objected fiercely to the presumed increased noise, although business aircraft already regularly used the airfield. John Selwyn Gummer, the Conservative environment secretary, blocked Filton's conversion in 1996 for no obvious reason other than to persuade the protesting residents to re-elect Michael Stern, the Tory MP for Bristol North-West. Stern claimed the airport 'would have stultified a considerable amount of housing development in an area where it is locally desired.' Stern nevertheless lost his seat in 1997, the year the council sold its majority stake in Lulsgate airport. Renamed Bristol International Airport, its ownership changed again in 2001 when Macquarie & Cintra acquired it for £198m. The fast expanding airport, with a new well-designed terminal and more air routes, had 3.8m passengers in 2003. But it still has neither motorway nor rail links.

Harbourside schemes

Despite their airport disagreement, BCCI and Bristol City Council formed a partnership to transform the dismal Canon's Marsh into a cultural, commercial and residential quarter. With the land being renamed Harbourside, a Harbourside Sponsors' Group was formed in 1993 initially with Diana Kershaw and later John Savage as its chair. BCCI and the council, which owned a substantial part of the 66 acres, brought together English Partnerships and other landowners on the site: Lloyds Bank, which became Lloyds TSB, British Gas, British Rail, Lattice Properties and JT Group. The same year, Bristol Cultural Development Partnership (BCDP) was set up, supported by BCCI and the council. Although a very small team led by Andrew Kelly, its role was to act as a catalyst and facilitator for cultural activities and to orchestrate bids for funding.

Arnolfini had another refurbishment that year, with JT involved in managing alterations and improvements. The bookshop moved to the ground floor and a new gallery and an education room were created upstairs. Most of the design work was by Roger Mortimer, who had by then retired from JT and joined Arnolfini's council of management. He contributed his knowledge of the building and property matters while trustees began to discuss future expansion within Bush House. Jeremy Fry had resigned as chair the previous year and was succeeded by Jonathan Harvey, a founder and co-director of Acme Studios in London. Acme was set up in 1972 as a non-profitmaking company to provide low-cost studios and living places for artists. It now manages more than 460 such places in East and South-east London, making it the largest provider of its kind in Britain.

Harbourside Sponsors' Group got underway after the consultants Drivers Jonas presented a development framework. Concept Planning Group, a joint venture between the architects Ferguson Mann, Alec French Partnership and Bruges Tozer, produced a viability plan. Subsequently Crosby Homes and Crest Nicholson were invited to join the sponsors' group when they were to develop parts of the site. Lloyds Bank, gratified that its headquarters would no longer be isolated, advertised in 1994 that Harbourside was 'a scheme which is set to turn a virtual wasteland in the heart of the city into a thriving business, cultural and residential centre.' John Pontin reported: 'There can be no doubt that our most significant property interests are located within the Harbourside redevelopment area.'

Bristol itself was becoming more united and confident. The development corporation had been scrapped and Avon County Council abolished in 1996, with the Bristol City Council formed as an unitary authority. An inspired joint venture was to celebrate the 500th anniversary of John Cabot's epic voyage in 1497 from Bristol to Newfoundland by constructing on the quayside a replica of his ship *Matthew*. The driving force behind this project was St. John Hartnell, who died in January, 2006. The replica – not an exact copy because the design of Cabot's square-rigged caravel was unknown – took part in an 'International Festival of the Sea' at the Floating Harbour in 1996, bringing many thousands of people to the waterfront. The following year, marking the anniversary, the ship sailed across the Atlantic to Newfoundland and the east coast of North America. She returned to Bristol, docking next to Brunel's ss *Great Britain* which was being restored.

Cultural advances on the waterfront were making the city more cosmopolitan. Arnolfini continued to present work by international artists and to attract visitors from around the country and abroad, as well as running education programmes with Bristol's communities. The Architecture Centre, founded by the Bristol Centre for the Advancement of Architecture, a charitable trust, was opened next to Bush House in 1996 to encourage public appreciation of the built environment. The first such centre to be set up outside London, it has a small exhibition gallery, a bookshop and meeting room and organises programmes and lectures. Near the Floating Harbour, the disused Brooke Bond tea-packing factory was converted to be called Spike Island, a co-operative venture with over 70 artists' studios, a large exhibitions hall and screenprinting workshops. David Johnstone, a director of JT Group, was a trustee and helped to initiate Spike Island in negotiations with Brooke Bond and drawing upon JT's skills. The artist-led scheme received one of the first lottery grants, with Peter Barker-Mill providing a principal source of matching funds.

On Harbourside, after long delays, there was the first new large-scale development since Lloyds TSB's headquarters. A £97m project to be named At-Bristol was the main visitor attraction. Grants came from the National Lottery Millennium Fund, the city council, South West of England Regional Development Agency (set up in 1999) and private sector partners. The scheme was a 'hands-on' interactive science centre called Explore, designed by Chris Wilkinson Architects, a natural history centre called Wildscreen World (now named Wildwalk), designed by Michael Hopkins & Partners, and an Imax cinema. A pedestrian square, called Millennium Square, was created above an underground car park built for 550 cars with light installations as part of a public arts programme. The square, with lottery funding, is a rare example in the country of new developments which allow, rather than restrict, free 24-hour public access. Some memories of the historic harbour survived within At-Bristol: a Victorian leadworks and a railway goods shed, built about 1900.

Setback and an advance

The waterfront was being revitalised while At-Bristol was built - it was to be opened to the public in July 2000. New apartments alongside the Floating Harbour encouraged people to live in the heart of the city. A world-class cultural asset was proposed: Harbourside Centre,

The proposed Harbourside Centre: scuppered when the Arts Council pulled out.

a 2,300-seat concert hall and a 450-seat dance theatre. The city council earmarked the site adjacent to JT's V-shed on the quay opposite to Arnolfini. The Arts Council provided £4.8m for design work and reserved £58m of lottery money to complete the scheme. After an international competition, Behnisch, Behnisch & Partner, the Stuttgart-based architectural firm, was chosen in 1997 for its 'exploding greenhouse' – a spectacular sculptural design in steel and glass.

In July 1998, there was a sudden reversal of policy at the Arts Council under its new management, which withdrew its support, claiming the project was 'flawed in many ways'. The *Western Daily Press*, headlining the story 'West's £89m dream in ruins,' wrote that there had been repeated clashes over the way the project was being handled with a 'bitter behind-the-scenes wrangle over the plans.'

At the same time, the Arts Council made a conciliatory gesture: 'it would approve its commitment to Bristol' by awarding a £317,000 grant to Arnolfini to plan its renovation with expansion of its galleries. This was to prepare a full-scale project, with a design team led by the architect Robin Snell of Snell Associates and the artist Susanna Heron, and which was to lead eventually to the transformation of its home at Bush House.

13 A bridge forward
Advances for Harbourside

Water and the arts are a powerful combination and nowhere offers that combination better than Bristol's Harbourside.
Anne White, city councillor (2003)

Many Bristolians regretted the Arts Council's rejection in 1998 of the proposed Harbourside Centre which would have been a landmark concert hall of national recognition. The disappointment could add to envy of Cardiff Bay's £106m slate-clad Millennium Centre, which opened with a 1,900-seat theatre in November 2004. For Harbourside, it was a serious setback, but other projects were to be brought forward on the waterfront to make it the liveliest part of the city.

As early as 1984, JT Group had proposed a footbridge to cross St Augustine's Reach, linking Arnolfini on the east side and Watershed Media Centre on the west. The city council owned the quaysides and funds were not then made available to carry out the project. A decade later, however, the scheme was reborn when JT wanted to renegotiate its leases of the U and V-sheds on St Augustine's Reach to convert them to bars and restaurants. To grant planning consent, the council required JT to pay for repairs to the walkways and to install a footbridge. This would be in JT's interests, since it would raise the commercial value of the leisure sheds when the public would be able to cross between the quaysides.

JT initiated the footbridge in 1994 with Arnolfini backing the idea that it should be designed by an artist in collaboration with the structural engineers. A design competition was held and the Irish sculptor Eilis O'Connell was commissioned. Ove Arup was selected as the engineers, Dew Construction as contractors, and David Abels, the Bristol boatbuilder which made the metal structure. Derek Salmon of JT was quoted in *Contract Journal* as saying: 'We were finally able to fund construction of the bridge after renegotiating with the city the leases we had on waterside buildings adjacent to where the bridge will span. That allowed us to attract the necessary finance, for which we sought assistance from English Partnerships.' He added: 'This bridge is a stunning collaboration between an artist, a boatbuilder and the construction industry. It is not being built directly from public funds, yet it will provide an extremely useful link for the public.'

Its cantilevered structure has a curved 3-metre wide walkway, with gentle gradients for disabled people and high, trumpet-shaped horns as counterweights to enable the bridge to swing open for yachts. The striking shape was denigrated in the *Bristol Evening Post* by a group of 11 architects and engineers. One architect described it as 'an architectural travesty that would completely destroy the historic character of a unique industrial site.' Another claimed that the design was more fitting to Disneyland.

Completed in 1999, it was named Pero's Bridge after an eighteenth-century slave owned by the Bristol sugar merchant John Pinney, who had plantations in the Caribbean. His handsome Bristol town house, built about 1790, and now known as The Georgian House, is open to the public. During the year when the bridge opened, the Pontin Charitable Trust funded Still Line, a sculpture for Castle Park in Bristol. The 2.5m stone and stainless steel sculpture, incorporating water, was by Ann Christopher, the Royal Academician who had studied at West of England College of Art. The Charitable Trust, together with two other trusts John Pontin had created with money generated by the JT business, was to donate over £1m to charitable causes by 2004.

Pero's Bridge designed by Ellis O'Connell and Ove Arup. The revamped U-shed is behind. Photo: Stephen Morris

The footbridge immediately became much appreciated by visitors, city workers and local residents in its link across St Augustine's Reach. It is part of the 'Millennium Mile' – the walkway from Temple Meads station, through the restored Queen Square, across the quays to the At-Bristol attractions and to the quayside opposite the ss *Great Britain*. The bridge is constantly photographed and regularly shown on local television and in tourist literature. The critics may have reconsidered.

While the bridge was being built, The Bush Consultancy, which had been set up by JT in 1989, was sold to its management team in December 1997. The consultancy, which later moved to a former church in St George, Bristol, has stated: 'Many of our projects include regeneration of sites or buildings and all commissions include consideration and integration of sustainable solutions.' JT meanwhile planned the redevelopment of the U and V transit sheds for leisure and entertainment. U-shed, together with V-shed had been used in the 1970s as Bristol Exhibition Centre, was structurally unsound and had to be demolished and rebuilt. The £1.6m development, designed by The Bush Consultancy and built by Dew Construction, was substantially let to Allied Domecq for use as a night club and with café-bars on the ground floor. The neighbouring V-shed was also designed by the consultancy and refurbished at a cost of £1.5m. It was handed over in June 2000 to trade as Lloyds No. 1 bar, Pitcher & Piano café-bar and Brannigans, which promoted itself for 'eating, dancing and cavorting.' Brannigans, however, ceased trading in 2004. Although all the converted sheds alongside St. Augustine's Reach are totally functional, their waterfront elevations have been complimented by an architectural writer for their 'rhythm and poetry'.

Change of board

John Pontin resigned as chairman in March 1998 for personal reasons, the long terminal illness of his wife. Sylviane, who was French, had a book of poetry published in 1997, called *Couleurs d'instants* (Delian Bower Publishing). John retained his controlling shareholding while David Johnstone took over as chairman. David said: 'His interest in our activities and all aspects of the preservation of the environment by sustainable development remains undiminished.' In the company's 1998 report, he stated: 'Having secured funding for our investment properties in Bristol Harbourside, our balance sheet ratios have been restored to acceptable levels. This gives the group a stable platform from which to complete the development of its remaining Harbourside interests and to seek new development opportunities in the future. The group is now constituted as a property investment and development group with no other trading interests.'

Tessa Jackson, who had been Arnolfini's director since 1991, left in autumn 1999 to be director of the Scottish Arts Council and later to be artistic director of Artes Mundi, the Wales International Visual Art Prize which was inaugurated in 2004. During Jackson's directorship in the 1990s, artists exhibiting at Arnolfini were, or were to become, some of the best-known. They included Mona Hatoum, Patrick Heron, Rachel Whiteread, Victor Burgin, Peter Blake, Tracey Emin, Peter Doig, Tracey Moffat and Gilbert and George. Caroline Collier, who was appointed as Arnolfini's director, in succession to Tessa, had been general manager of the modernist De La Warr Pavilion at Bexhill, East Sussex, and responsible for its restoration and development.

John Pontin rejoined the board as chairman in May 2000, with David as deputy chairman. John's son Ben, a senior lecturer in environmental law at the University of the West of England, joined as a non-executive director while Ivor Stolliday, and Christopher Zealley remained as non-executive directors and Tim Miles as board secretary. That May, John was interviewed by *Bristol Evening Post* under the headline 'One man's dream is coming true' about the transformation of the docklands. He was quoted as recalling: 'We were fascinated by the docks and strongly believed that the area would come back into its own with the right kind of development. Even then, we were great believers in urban renewal and recycling old buildings.'

JT had not, however, sought to prepare a masterplan for Harbourside. 'Although we had great visions for the docks, we could never have imagined how waterfront areas were going to become such culturally vibrant places,' John said. 'The influence of European developments at places like Barcelona has had a tremendous impact. Developers in the 1980s would have possibly put a shopping precinct on Canon's Marsh and maybe a few houses. Clearly it needs something far more imaginative than that, if only to tie in and complement the other developments, like the At-Bristol architecture and our own buildings.'

South Building

A new development on the Harbourside was initiated by JT Group and completed in April 2001, a mixed-use £1.8m South Building overlooking both Millennium Square and Anchor Square. Designed by Alec French Partnership, it has a covered arcade and a curved metal roof, supported by tall wooden masts to reflect Bristol's maritime history. Kier Western, based in Bristol and part of Kier Group, was contracted by JT to construct the shell for themed restaurant/bars for Scottish & Newcastle. In June 2001, Scottish & Newcastle decided to pull out of retailing there and agreed to sell the lease to Luminar Leisure, already a tenant of W-shed, which was to make it a multi-themed venue.

Harbourside led the trend for large mixed-use developments, combining work, living and leisure. This was in contrast to the city's historic quarters which were distinctly for separate business, retail or residential use. The next, but long-delayed, development was by Crest Nicholson on 16 acres of the remaining derelict land. Its initial design in 1998 provoked local protests against ugly buildings and spoilt views. A rival plan was put forward the next year by the architect George Ferguson, of Ferguson Mann. Ferguson had converted a disused cigarette factory in south Bristol to include a performance arts centre, named Tobacco Factory. (He was elected president of RIBA for 2003-05) His 'Little Venice' scheme was based on the principles of 'urban renaissance.' A revised proposal by Crest Nicholson followed but the city council's planning committee voted against it in January 2000.

That summer, Crest Nicholson appointed Edward Cullinan Architects, based in London, to devise a new masterplan including elements of the Ferguson Mann scheme. Edward Cullinan described the plan as 'being organised around new and improved public spaces, providing over four acres of accessible landscape.' A meeting was called by the Friends of Canon's Marsh, attended by over 300 people, who opposed the plan. Councillors, however, voted unanimously in favour.

Detailed proposals were put forward in 2003, with the project encouraged by the bank HBOS which wanted the headquarters of its subsidiary Clerical Medical to be built on the waterfront, next to Lloyds TSB. It was designed by the Bristol-based architects Fitzroy Robinson. The Crest Nicholson scheme, with Bristol landscape architects Grant Associates and engineers Ove Arup, featured promenades, a small inlet for boats, restaurants, bars and flats, including an eight-storey split rotunda. A leisure building and hotel was designed by architects Faulkner Brown, with restaurants, cafés and a supermarket on the ground level and a fitness centre and casino on the upper level.

Arnolfini's future

In autumn 2001, the Arts Council, having made its earlier £317,000 grant to plan Arnolfini's redevelopment, provided a £7.5m grant through the national lottery. The grant enabled Arnolfini to acquire the freehold of Bush House from the landlord Ivory Gate (UK) for £6.25m. The overall budget for the redevelopment, including the purchase, was £12m.

Nicholas Serota, director of Tate, became Arnolfini's project champion. 'Since 1961 Arnolfini has built an international reputation as a centre for the arts founded on visual awareness,' he said. 'This scheme will give Arnolfini a permanent home and facilities which ensure the continuing excellence of its programme.' In November 2001, a big celebration of 400 people was held at Arnolfini to mark its joint 40th anniversary with JT, which sponsored the party, and with Serota and John Pontin making speeches to credit the past and future.

The project was financially supported by Arts Council England's capital services, Arts Council England South West, the city council and South West Regional Development Agency. Contributions included money from Arnolfini's endowment fund and collection trust; Ankerdene Trust; Garfield Weston Foundation; Henry Moore Foundation; Pilgrim Trust; the Society of Merchant Venturers and TLT Solicitors, who were Bush House tenants. An Arnolfini fundraising subcommittee included John Pontin.

Bristol at this time was one of six British cities shortlisted to be the 2008 European Capital of Culture, with Bristol Cultural Development Partnership organising the bid, led by Andrew Kelly and Nicky Rylance, then deputy chief executive of Bristol Chamber of

Commerce & Initiative. The bid sought to embrace a kaleidoscopic range of cultural activities. It was also linked to Legible City, a signage project to show safe pedestrian routes and to encourage more use of public transport in the city congested with cars. Anthony Sampson, author of Anatomy of Britain and its later editions, wrote in *The Independent* (July 1 2004): 'British cities are disintegrating and being replaced by American-type 'edge cities' totally dependent on cars, with long-term social and environmental costs which are incalculable.'

One short stretch of motorway – the M32 into the centre of Bristol – was criticised by the 2008 judging panel because of the way it split the urban districts. This was apparently a factor in failing to win the title despite praise for the city. Jeremy Isaacs, the panel's chairman, said: 'Some people thought Bristol had the most European feel of all the cities we went to, because of the good things it has done at the waterfront…it's a wonderful place to go to, we were very impressed with Bristol.' But there were other disadvantages than the M32 – not least the aborted Harbourside Centre and the lack of a modern stadium (while Cardiff had its new millennium stadium with a retractable roof). Bristol's waterfront, with so many bars, could also suffer from persistent night-time 'binge drinking' – although any British city would be vulnerable to alcoholic violence. To combat anti-social behaviour, the council and police launched a joint drive in 2004 for a street-drinking ban, including Harbourside.

Liverpool, in 2003, won the award for 2008 European Capital of Culture while the government named the shortlisted cities as Centres of Culture. (Tessa Jowell, the culture secretary, presented Bristol's certificate at an informal ceremony at Arnolfini) The ongoing rejuvenation of the waterfront remained crucial. The city council recognised the pioneering effect of Arnolfini and Watershed: 'These two developments,' its website stated, 'were critical in Bristol's repositioning as a major cultural centre, recognised by our designation as a centre of excellence during the city's bid for the 2008 European Capital of Culture.' It added: 'The city once again looks to one of its greatest assets, the Harbourside as the true heart of the city.'

Prince Street home

Arnolfini, when expecting to need more office space, had previously bought 70 Prince Street next to Bush House. It was one of three Georgian terraced properties which had been a tea and spice merchant's house. The building was acquired from JT, which had bought it in 1980 and renovated it when it was close to collapse. Arnolfini, after buying Bush House and so being able to expand within it, sold 70 Prince Street back to JT which, in April 2003, moved out of Bush House to have the Georgian property as its headquarters.

With the Arts Council England grant, Arnolfini, chaired by Jonathan Harvey and directed by Caroline Collier, was now able to plan a much more ambitious design by Robin Snell and Susanna Heron. Snell Associates' past projects included the art gallery for Surrey Institute of Art and Design, a new stadium for Fulham Football Club, the Northern Architecture Exhibition Centre at Newcastle, and the redevelopment of the Theatre Royal, Gibraltar. Heron has worked on many public commissions – one of which was Side Street, a covered pedestrian street opened in central London in 2003. Arnolfini's project manager was John Monahan, the founder of Bishopston Estates and Management, a Bath-based project management company. His work had included the Wiltshire Music Centre at Bradford-upon-Avon.

As Arnolfini's design plans proceeded, its programmes continued with experimental visual and live performance art, as well as its cinema. In 2002, it curated Listen to Britain, a touring exhibition by Victor Burgin, an internationally recognised originator of conceptual art of moving and still images. That year, Deanna Petherbridge, an artist known for pen-and-ink drawing with architectural, social and political themes, was appointed the first Arnolfini research professor of drawing at the University of the West of England. Other programmes – described in the rather hackneyed phrase as 'cutting edge' – included Breathing Space, a series of commissions by local and international artists, Inbetween Time, which was Arnolfini's first festival of live art, and Fresh Today, a live art project involving a group of disabled artists from the Bristol organisation Art+Power.

Bush House transformed

In autumn 2003, Arnolfini closed its galleries and public spaces with the building work ready to begin at a cost of some £6m. It was to create a fresh environment for its programme of new and experimental visual arts, live art, performance, dance, film, literature and music. Cowlin Construction, based in Bristol, was chosen as the main contractor. Established in 1834, it is one of the UK's leading privately owned construction companies and considered itself at the forefront of partnering principles. Cowlin, it stated, 'has an enviable reputation in the design and build sector, having successfully completed a broad range of projects under this type of contract over many years.' Cowlin was not, though, rebuilding Bush House in the design and build method. The quantity surveyors were Gardiner & Theobold and Ove Arup were engineers for the structural, mechanical and electrical elements with lighting, acoustics and fire protection.

With the re-opening in autumn 2005 – 30 years after JT and Arnolfini moved into Bush House – the lengthy timetable was needed to carry out substantial structural and engineering work. As always, construction work in an existing building would be more complex and difficult than to erect a new building. Arnolfini, housed on the ground and first floors, expanded into the second floor and basement. The work included digging out the basement, protected below the water level, to provide public facilities including toilets. A central reception area was made as a clear layout for visitors and a lift shaft through four storeys. The lift was a key element because Arnolfini, lacking a lift, had restricted access for disabled visitors.

Most dramatically, a large double-height gallery was created, without obstructive pillars, which had been dismantled. Other parts of the reconstruction were improved gallery spaces, an education centre, library archive, 60-seat studio, and the redesigned bookshop and café-bar. Climatic controls were installed to preserve delicate works of arts and to make the galleries much more comfortable for staff and visitors. Admission to the building remained free. The three upper floors were rented, providing income to aid Arnolfini's financial sustainability. Its 'full house' tenants were the University of the West of England, the consulting engineers Faber Maunsell and On Demand Distribution (OD2), Europe's leading digital distributor of music. OD2's co-founder was Peter Gabriel, the musician who had been with the band Genesis.

During the building work, Arnolfini kept open its bookshop, moving it to a temporary cabin on the quayside. An outreach programme of events, called Interlude, was arranged throughout the construction period. In February 2004, as one of the events, it brought to Bristol a programme called Wonderful: Visions of the Near Future. The collaborations between artists and scientists were held in the Industrial Museum opposite Bush House and live art events were commissioned by Arnolfini. A video project Out of Site was for five young people, recruited through Education Unlimited and with the artist Kathleen Herbert. Education Unlimited had been initiated by John Savage as chair of the West of England's Learning and Skills Council. The project was to observe the labour and craft of the rebuilding, including filming a recycling centre where the skips of rubble had been brought for re-use or landfill. Another programme was Inaudible City, an audio work by Zoe Irvine to record outdoor conversations about the city's building developments.

On a summer's day in 2004, Jeremy Rees' life was marked by a ceremony at Arnolfini in the new double-height gallery as it was being constructed – with eight graffiti artists brought into the gallery, during a weekend of Bristol's Architecture Week, for what was a 'fleeting installation' of Talking Walls. Nearly 200 people came, many of them artists, curators and art teachers. The guests included Jeremy's widow Annabel as well as Adam, the son of Peter Barker-Mill who had chaired Arnolfini and provided its endowment funds, and John Pontin. Speeches to celebrate Jeremy's achievements were made by Nicholas Serota and Simon Cook, the Lord Mayor of Bristol who, as a councillor was also a trustee of Arnolfini. There followed a visit to the Forest of Dean, to walk through the beguiling sculpture trail of which Jeremy had been a founder and trustee.

Revamped Watershed

Watershed Media Centre, which had nearly half a million visitors in 2004, has itself been revamped. It was, its website stated, 'an investment programme designed to keep Watershed fresh and looking to the future.' It stayed open during the redevelopment, funded by Arts Council England, Bristol City Council, South-west Regional Development Agency and the University of the West of England. A third cinema opened in 2004 to provide bigger audiences for its independent films and to have more capacity for events. Its original two cinemas were refurbished and other facilities redesigned, including a new lift and a bigger café-bar.

JT remains the landlord of its two connected sheds on a long lease. The centre continues to specialise in film, hosting the short-film festivals Brief Encounters and Animated Encounters. It also explores digital technologies including an online project called Electric December, an annual festive programme to include video, multimedia and visual arts. It claims: 'Creativity and difference are the cornerstones of the Watershed brand, extending choice and cultural diversity.' A creative web project, reflecting on the issues raised at the Rio Earth Summit in 1992, featured work by children from four local primary schools. The project, which went live on the eve of the 2002 Johannesburg world summit on sustainable development, was supported by the Pontin Charitable Trust.

'This massive investment in Arnolfini and Watershed will help establish Harbourside as a unique cultural and creative industries quarter to match the best in Europe,' Anne White, a city councillor, said in August 2003. Plans were underway to transform the quayside's Industrial Museum into the Museum of Bristol, to illustrate the city's past role as one of the country's great ports. It is hoped to open in 2009. Within reach of Harbourside are other cultural attractions: the much-improved Royal West of England Academy, the renovated St George's concert hall, the City Museum & Art Gallery in its Edwardian Baroque building and which celebrated its 100th anniversary in 2005, Tobacco Factory with its theatre, and the Old Vic, the country's earliest surviving theatre. The British Empire & Commonwealth Museum opened in 2002 at Brunel's original Temple Meads station. Next to the station and Temple Quarter, where a new commercial centre has been built, South West RDA and the city council planned a 10,000-seat multi-purpose arena intended to be ready in 2008.

Arnolfini, reopened in autumn 2005, intended its innovative artistic programme 'to reinforce its values as a place for everybody to share the pleasures and creative dissonances of the art of our time – a public space for the imagination to take flight.' Caroline Collier, its director, emphasised how important it was to have a dynamic relationship with the city and its arts activity, with Arnolfini maintaining its 'relative intimacy' as a meeting point and crossing place for the eclectic variety of arts.

Many thousands came to Arnolfini as it reopened with its exhibition 'This storm is what we call progress'. It was to be a celebration and commemoration with an international group show which included Jyll Bradley's installation of cut flowers, its selection helped by Bristol people. Annabel Rees, in memory of her husband Jeremy, chose the painting by JMW Turner *Norham Castle Sunrise*, starting a new day and a new Arnolfini. The climate control protected such a valuable and delicate picture, which it would not have previously been possible to show in the galleries. A little book to mark the opening was *Arnolfini: Art Spaces*, published by Scala, and the *Architectural Review* said the construction was 'a welcome return to the city's vibrant cultural scene'. As Nicholas Serota, Tate director, said in *The Guardian*, the refurbishment allowed Arnolfini to 'take its place as one of a handful of the most significant contemporary cultural centres in Europe.'

Tom Trevor, who had been a director of the contemporary Spacex Gallery in Exeter, became Arnolfini's director in October 2005, after Caroline Collier had been appointed Tate's head of national initiatives. 'Arnolfini', she said, 'would be a continuation of a pioneering and progressive spirit.' The next exhibition, shown from November until mid-January 2006, was 'Starting at Zero: Black Mountain College 1933-57', and the project 'Playing John Cage'. It was the first exhibition in the UK of the Black Mountain College which had been avant-garde art in America. The remarkable range from the college's works of art and documentation was seen in the now bigger spaces in Arnolfini, now enhancing its contemporary arts and education programmes and seeking to embrace wider audiences.

Creative Bristol (an initiative of Bristol Cultural Development Partnership) aimed to resurrect many of the projects put forward in the Capital of Culture bid, as well as a festival to celebrate the double centenary of Brunel in 2006. Brunel's inspirational works – Clifton suspension bridge, the old station at Temple Meads and ss *Great Britain* – are still today among the best symbols of Bristol, while the Floating Harbour itself is a transformation. The Harbourside Sponsors' Group claimed that the waterfront was 'undergoing a cultural renaissance that will firmly establish it as one of Europe's leading quarters for the arts and creative industries.'

14 Sustaining the environment
Act locally, change globally

In industrialised countries, the consumption patterns of cities are placing severe stress on the global ecosystem...Countries need to take a more integrated approach to development, with high priority being given to the needs of the urban and rural poor.

UN Division for Sustainable Development (2004)

When JT Group was founded, in 1961, it was no more likely than any other construction company to prioritise the sustainable practices which require an optimum standard of insulation, reduction of waste and recycling of materials. In the post-war era, developers were little concerned about environmental matters when the huge demand was for slum clearance, replacement of bombed buildings, new council housing and commercial property schemes. The pressure groups Greenpeace and the British arm of the Friends of the Earth were not initiated until 1971.

Until the late twentieth century, there had been minimal debate in any countries about how human activities were affecting the environment. It was the book *Silent Spring* (1962) by the American author Rachel Carson, detailing the dangers of chemical pesticides such as DDT, which was to have a worldwide influence on the awareness of science's impact on human, animal and plant life. This led to a birth of environmental movements. It was not, though, until 1988 that the Intergovernmental Panel on Climate Change (IPCC) was set up by the World Meteorological Organisation and United Nations Environment Programme. The following year, the Conservative government hosted a conference on 'Saving the ozone layer' to put climate change on the UK's political agenda.

Although JT was always run as a competitive, cost-conscious business, John Pontin's personal interest in environmental issues and sustainable development steadily influenced the company's attitude to construction, in which the industry should accept great responsibility for the use of energy and resources, both for new building work and maintenance. Cement production, the mainstay of construction, is a major source of greenhouse gas emissions. JT endorsed a green policy in its use of materials by seeking, for example, to avoid CFCs (chlorofluorocarbons), urea formaldehyde foam insulation and timber from non-sustainable sources.

'The group is encouraging a responsible approach to environmental matters in all its activities,' John reported in November 1991. 'In particular, JT Design Build has recognised its major role in this aspect of business policy and has recently carried out a complete environmental audit of its practices. This has already led to an effective 'green policy' which is being progressively implemented internally. It has attracted considerable interest from existing and prospective clients for its design build services.'

In October 1992, JT organised an environmental conference – endorsed by the Confederation of British Industry, Business in the Environment and the Institute of Directors – at Watershed Media Centre. 'This event is part of our committed campaign to put the environment on the agenda for businesses,' JT stated. Representatives of over 120 firms and organisations attended. JT published, jointly with Ove Arup & Partners, *The Green Construction Handbook: A Manual for Clients and Construction Professionals.* JT also published Going Green, a guide introduced by Richard Demery and written by Simon Miller to achieve more environmentally friendly buildings, which received a DTI award.

'Everyone is talking about the environment,' Simon Miller wrote. 'However, what the majority of people do not realise is the contribution that 'Green Buildings' can make to improving our environmental performance. Currently, within the UK, buildings use over half the energy consumed in the country.' He concluded: 'In the future, buildings must become more environmentally friendly. This will be partly driven through statutory regulations but public opinion and rising energy costs will soon become a potent incentive to improve the situation. This is not a passing fad; as natural resources run out we will have no choice but to adopt these principles.'

Population explosion

Ever since the dawn of human civilisation, the Earth's atmosphere had been relatively benign despite perennial setbacks to communities through natural acts: earthquakes, volcanic eruptions, hurricanes, floods and heatwaves. It is only since the Industrial Revolution, and especially within recent decades, that there has been a profound transformation of the environment, affected less by natural forces and much more by the impact of the fast-rising global population, with an exponential increase in energy usage and consumption. A century ago, the world population was merely 1.6bn and the UK was estimated to have 38 million people. Since then, the British population has risen to about 60 million. A study by the London School of Economics reported in December 2004 that ethnic minority groups accounted for nearly three-quarters of Britain's population growth between 1991 and 2001, with the total UK population rising by 4 per cent in the decade. The Office of National Statistics calculates that, with immigration and longer life expectancy being the chief factors, numbers in Britain will reach nearly 65 million by 2025. World population since 1900 has quadrupled to over 6bn, rising most sharply since the Second World War with birth rates falling but death rates declining even faster. There is now estimated to be a net increase of 78 million people a year, creating a population within every two days to be equivalent to the size of Bristol.

England itself has long been one of the most crowded countries. In the South-west, its most densely populated area is the former Avon county encompassing Bristol, with close to one million people – an average of 740 people in every square kilometre. Worldwide, the fastest growth is mostly in the poorest regions although numbers in the United States have escalated from 200 million in 1981 to 294 million in 2004. The multiplying humans require ever more supplies of food, water and energy. Farming lands are destroyed by soil erosion and desertification (degradation of formerly productive land) and oceans are overfished. Ecology – the relationship between living things and their surroundings – shows that animals and plants are losing wild habitats and thousands of species become extinct every year. The United States, the leading industrialised nation, is the prime polluter, while less developed nations also cause pollution with agricultural 'slash and burning' and under-regulated industries which lack emission controls.

Vulnerable world

The Earth radiates the sun's heat back into space with carbon dioxide and other gases trapping some of the outgoing heat. Without this 'greenhouse effect', temperatures would be much lower and the planet would not be hospitable. However, the burning of fossil fuels, deforestation, motor and air transport and manufactures spawned much greater quantities of carbon dioxide and methane. Global surface temperatures heightened during the twentieth century, with the 10 warmest years in its last 15 years. In 2001, the IPCC forecast that carbon dioxide, surface temperatures, precipitation and sea level were all projected to increase globally during the twenty first century because of human activities. It predicted that the sea level would rise by between 11cm and 77cm by 2100.

National and international politicians were slow to respond to climate instability. After the airborne attack on New York and Washington on September 11 2001, British and US political leaders concentrated on a nebulous 'war on terrorism', rather than promoting policies to mitigate damage to the environment. The UN's Kyoto protocol, signed by nations from 1998, was an agreement that industrialised nations should reduce greenhouse gas emissions by cutting dependence on fossil fuels. Russia eventually ratified the protocol in autumn 2004 but the US and Australian governments failed to support the agreement. The US has only four per cent of the world's population but generates a quarter of the greenhouse gas emissions. David King, the UK government's chief scientist, stated in his article published in the American journal *Science* in 2004 that 'In my view, climate change is the most severe problem we are facing today, more serious even than the threat of terrorism.' At a climate change conference at Exeter in February 2005, he said there was a consensus among scientists that there was a 'globally serious and urgent issue on which we need to take action.' Action, for example, could be to pump carbon dioxide underground.

Although changes in human behaviour might slow the rate of global warming, it requires considerable reductions in emissions to stabilise the climate. Scientists calculate that carbon dioxide, once released into the atmosphere, remains there for about 100 years. Forecasts for global energy have been estimated by the International Energy Agency to rise by almost 60 per cent from 2002 to 2030. Burning fossil fuels is bound to intensify climate change. Glaciers and icecaps are melting, sea levels rising and in Britain the winters are warmer and wetter. With many of the world's cities having evolved from trading ports, conurbations close to sea level are ever more vulnerable. The Thames Barrier has been essential to prevent flooding in London. Many parts of the UK have the risk of rivers overflowing when heavy rainfall causes an immediate run-off because so much land has been surfaced with buildings, roads, car parks and domestic paving.

Solar power

Not until September 2004 did the British prime minister make a major speech on global warming. Tony Blair said climate change had the potential to unleash a human and economic catastrophe if left unchecked and he spoke of the need for a 'green industrial revolution' of energy-efficient and sustainable developments. But in November, George W. Bush was re-elected as US president and continued not to accept the Kyoto protocol. Blair, at the World Economic Forum in January 2005, became much more politically cautious. He said climate change was not universally accepted and evidence was disputed. He argued that global warming could be tackled without enormous economic cost through more intelligent use of science, a greater contribution by rapidly developing economies and market mechanisms such as emissions trading.

During the same month, the government published plans to build as many as 1.1 million homes in London and the South-east over a 20-year period. A report then by the parliamentary environmental audit committee criticised the government for its non-environmental policies for new housing which would exacerbate climate change. The committee also criticised property developers for an 'apparent reluctance of the industry to recognise the need for drastic improvement in how homes are built.' In March 2005, the committee criticised the government for 'creating the appearance of activity' while 'evading the harder national and international political decisions.' Later that month, Kofi Annan, secretary-general of the UN, said an international study of the Millennium Ecosystem Assessment 'shows how human activities are causing environmental damage on a massive scale throughout the world, and how biodiversity – the very basis for life on Earth – is declining at an alarming rate.'

The UK government has estimated that energy used in homes could be cut by half by current technologies. Blair, on the same day of his September 2004 speech, had visited the Solarcentury company in London to see its solar panels with which photovoltaic cells produce electricity directly from sunlight. Jeremy Leggett, Solarcentury's chief executive, said: 'Solar photovoltaic roofs and facades on buildings give you high value insurance against rising future energy prices at increasingly low cost right where you need the energy. We can power much of the country and do so much faster than most people realise.'

John Pontin, in his dedication to support sustainability, had already commissioned Solarcentury to install solar-powered roofing at his own house, which had been designed by Roger Mortimer. At a cost of £27,000, the sunslates, replacing the original roof slates, produced power converted to the house's mains electricity with no emission of carbon dioxide. Dr Daniel Davies, Solarcentury's chief engineer, said it was the first sunslate installation in the UK by a non-specialist roofing contractor 'which demonstrated that photovoltaics could be easily installed on the millions of homes being built across the UK today.' John commented: 'I just had to get my lifestyle to fit in with my beliefs. By doing so, I am making my own contribution to a sustainable future. We cannot go on living by burning fossil fuels. We are spoiling our planet and the clean solution for tomorrow is the power from the sun.'

Renewable energy

In Britain, the main sources of renewable energy are wind (onshore and offshore), the sun (solar photovoltaic cells), water (conventional hydro systems and the technologies of tides and waves) and biomass (including energy crops.) These sources generated less than 3 per cent of the country's total electricity supply in 2004, with just 15 per cent of that produced by wind power. The government announced a target for renewable power to achieve 15 per cent of electricity requirements by 2015. Wind energy could meet these targets, as the UK is the windiest country in Europe with the potential to meet all of the country's electricity demands at relatively low cost. Over a thousand turbines have been erected but cause justifiable protests when installed on the most beautiful landscapes such as in Cornwall and Wales. Offshore turbines are beginning to be installed but at higher cost.

Britain's nuclear power stations, which in their early days were wrongly expected to produce unlimited cheap electricity, have not been replaced in the wake of the 1986 Chernobyl disaster in the Ukraine. With plutonium adding to fears of security risks, they are being decommissioned. Zac Goldsmith, editor of *The Ecologist*, opposed nuclear power in a published debate with James Lovelock, creator of the Gaia theory (*The Independent*, August 28 2004). He wrote: 'Whole villages in Britain's West Country are on the verge of being powered by environmentally benign small hydro projects. Biomass is emerging as the answer for others. Solar power is becoming cheaper by the year, and more efficient.'

Lovelock argued: 'No source of power is entirely safe, even windmills are not free of fatal accidents, but compared to nuclear power, the dangers of continuing to burn fossil fuels (oil, gas, coal) as our main energy source are far greater and they threaten not just individuals but civilisation itself…At least in the short term, alternative sources of energy remain wildly uneconomical…I hope it is not too late for the world to emulate France and make nuclear power our principal source of energy. At present we have no other viable alternative.'

An encouraging analysis by scientists at Princeton University in New Jersey in 2004 stated that work on implementing existing technologies could begin immediately in halting the escalation of global warming. The scientists identified 15 technologies – from wind, solar and nuclear energy to conservation techniques – that could have large-scale use, each solving a significant portion of the problem. Their analysis, published in Science in August 2004, indicated that many combinations of these technologies could prevent global emissions of greenhouse gases from rising for the next five decades.

Stephen Pacala and Robert Socolow, the professors who conducted the study, said that their analysis countered the common argument that a major new technology needed to be developed before greenhouse gases could be controlled. 'It certainly explodes the idea that we need to do research for a long time before getting started,' said Pacala, co-director with Socolow of Princeton's Carbon Mitigation Initiative. Socolow said: 'If we decide to act, we will need to reduce carbon emissions across the whole global economy. Fortunately, we have the tools to do this, especially if we think in terms of 50-year campaigns, not instant solutions.'

The UK's Carbon Trust, which works with businesses and the public sector to help reduce carbon emissions, states: 'Companies often worry that environmental concerns can hurt their profitability. In fact, it is more likely to be beneficial, with no-cost or low-cost measures producing energy savings.'

Where to build

Environmental policies, encouraged by national organisations including Friends of the Earth, have slowly gained more impact in Whitehall. The government-funded Construction Best Practice Programme, with its document *Building a better quality of life – A strategy for more sustainable construction* (April 2000) set out how the government wanted the construction industry to respond. The strategy, supported by the Chartered Institute of Building, intended to be a catalyst for change in the way buildings and infrastructure are designed, procured, constructed, maintained and used. Sir Martin Laing, launching a report by the Sustainable Construction Focus Group, said: 'We have tried to show what sustainability means in practical terms and what people can be doing now to become more sustainable. It is not rocket science. Nor does it conflict with other business objectives.'

Absurdly, the government charged value-added tax for repairs and renovation of existing houses but zero tax for new construction. 'VAT could be a powerful tool in pushing markets in a more sustainable direction,' wrote Roger Cowe and Jonathon Porritt (*Government's Business – Enabling corporate sustainability, Forum for the Future*, 2002). 'As a starter, the VAT system must never encourage the less sustainable alternative, as it does by favouring new housebuilding compared to renovation.' Recent targets were set by the government to have 60 per cent of all new houses built on brownfield sites to relieve the pressure on the rural countryside. But government studies indicated that up to half a million homes could be built on greenfield land in four southern areas during the next 30 years. 'Further countryside will be consumed to provide the roads, workplaces and shops associated with all those new houses and cars,' stated the Campaign to Protect Rural England (CPRE), arguing that the government should apply five sustainability tests:

1. Environmental capacity: New housebuilding should be tested regionally and locally against environmental capacity constraints, rather than imposed as targets from the top down.
2. Better use of resources: Development must make much better use of land and other natural resources, such as energy and minerals. Sprawling housing estates disconnected from jobs and services that waste land and generate traffic should not be allowed.
3. Redevelopment of brownfield sites: There should be higher targets for their re-use.
4. Even regions: There should be a coherent government strategy to share prosperity across all regions in England and reduce regional disparities.
5. Public involvement: There should be genuine opportunities for the public to have a say in decisions on new development in their area.

Zero Waste

In 2004, a West of England group took part in the 'Coffeehouse Challenge' of the Royal Society of Arts (RSA), marking its 250th anniversary, the society's first meeting having been in a coffeehouse at Covent Garden. Nationwide, groups promoted schemes for the society to select and support tangible projects. The West of England group, led by John Pontin, decided on the concept of zero waste, setting up a co-ordinating body 'to provide information, links and networks to generate and support action.' With an initial punchy slogan 'Cut the carbon', the West of England group was chosen by the RSA as one of six national winning projects with financial support for the next six years.

Naming itself as dCarb West, the group drew on partner organisations: Business West, the organisation which evolved from Bristol Chamber of Commerce & Initiative; Avon

Wildlife Trust; the Centre for Sustainable Energy; Envolve, previously called Bath Environment Centre and with John a board member, and the Recycling Consortium which offers advice and services in waste reduction. Throughout the country, huge amounts of waste are caused by consumer materialism and excessive packaging by manufacturers and retailers, but recycling has been a feeble effort by local authorities in comparison with countries such as Germany, France and Norway. In 1996 the Tory government introduced a landfill tax to reduce rubbish and encourage waste management techniques. But in the twenty first century as much as 85 per cent of the nation's waste is dumped into landfill sites. Ever fewer sites are to be selected to have minimal social and environmental impact. Bath & North East Somerset Council was one of the few local authorities which reached a recycling and composting rate of 29 per cent of household waste in 2003/04.

The Recycling Consortium is based at the Create Centre, next to Bristol's Cumberland Basin. Originally a bonded warehouse, close to the Floating Harbour, its massive cube-shaped redbrick structure was converted in 1994 as an environment centre. The conversion was designed by The Bush Consultancy, then part of JT. The centre is owned and run by Bristol City Council, hosting its sustainable development teams. It is also the home of the Local Agenda 21, one of the community-led groups set up internationally after being urged by the 1992 Earth Summit to 'think globally, act locally.'

That slogan was adapted by dCarb West as 'act locally, change globally.' Discussions about the Coffeehouse Challenge attracted interest in the village of Chew Magna, eight miles south of Bristol, and where John Pontin lives. It was proposed to reduce local energy wastage initially by 20 per cent and towards a carbon neutral community by the year 2020. The ultimate aim was to make Chew Magna the first village in the UK to be run entirely from sustainable energy sources. Ian Roderick, who chairs the scheme, wrote in the *Chew Valley Gazette*: 'This project aims to transform our region into one that is truly sustainable, one that wastes nothing – materials, energy or the spirit of the people who live here.'

To advance the project, JT bought a derelict stone-built mill in Chew Magna in 2005. 'There was a lot of interest and commitment in the village and it seemed as if the mill could be acquired as a physical resource and an information centre around the zero waste project,' he said. 'There are all sorts of ideas and there will be a community base from which to work.' Originally a flour mill on the river Chew with a surviving waterwheel, it was in a 'raw state, but such an iconic building.' *The Gazette* in April 2005, headlining 'Chew Mill to showcase Zero Waste project,' stated that John was 'at pains to avoid any assumption that this is 'his' project, and he points to the enthusiastic involvement of at least 60 Chew Magna residents already.'

In a questionnaire, villagers were asked to consider how the mill could be maximised for personal benefit and for the community as a whole. Ideas were floated to conceive

Chew Magna Mill, part of the Zero Waste project.

interactive education, exhibitions, information about energy saving and renewable energy methods, a café with local produce, a conference room or auditorium, a gym which might produce renewable energy and a recycling collection point. An open meeting in Chew Magna presented the project and four groups were formed as: Energy and transport; Waste and recycling; Consumption and people, particularly for local food; and Converging World, to link with other countries.

JT Group, acting as a 'friendly bank', financially supported the mill's purchase of nearly £500,000 before rebuild costs. It is hoped that the mill's environmental activities will gain charitable status. With its commitment to sustainability, JT had already created a new company in 2004 as a sensitive developer and which could support the mill's transformation. The company has an evocative name: Under the Sky.

15 A view to the future
JT's new company for urban regeneration

Business can find its challenge for our times: they provide the new community.
Karl-Henrik Robèrt (*The Natural Step Story*, New Society Publishers, 2002)

Two international organisations which seek to promote an environmentally friendly future, and with which John Pontin has stayed closely associated for many years, are Schumacher UK and The Natural Step. Their influence encouraged John, with JT Group's full support, to set up the company named Under the Sky as a not-for-profit company for urban regeneration and social enterprise to be a pioneer in the West of England.

Schumacher UK, the society founded in 1978 shortly after the death of Dr E.F. Schumacher, encourages alternative thinking and human-scale sustainable development, often in conflict with government policies. Schumacher, born in Germany and a Rhodes scholar at Oxford, was for 20 years the chief economic adviser to the National Coal Board. He advocated production from local resources for local needs to be the most rational way of economic life. The society's council members in 2005 include:

Satish Kumar, its president, editor of *Resurgence* magazine and director of
programmes at Schumacher College, Dartington.
John Pontin, vice-president.
Herbert Girardet, chairman, an author, film-maker and consultant on creating
sustainable cities and an honorary fellow of the RIBA.
Richard St. George, director, an environmental scientist and consultant, and member
of Sustainable Futures Group at Bristol University.
Diana Schumacher, writer and lecturer on ethics and the environment.
Simon Cooper, who had been public affairs director of GWR Group and is a trustee
of the Demos think-tank.

'Economic globalisation has expanded everywhere to the detriment of local democratic self-determination,' according to Schumacher UK. 'Local ecosystems, economies and communities have been gravely undermined by these trends. Even sustainable development, a concept that has become prominent in recent years, has tended to ignore the concerns of people in their neighbourhoods and communities.

'Schumacher UK,' it added, 'exists to challenge such developments and to propose alternatives. It provides a unique forum for promoting human scale solutions to the social and environmental problems facing us...Our primary function is to promote, generate and distribute concepts and processes that enable individuals and communities to take steps towards creating a sustainable future.'

The society, based at Bristol's Create Centre, formed the Schumacher Circle as a network of organisations inspired by Dr Schumacher's vision and to co-operate informally with each others' work. Together with the society, these are:

Schumacher College, Dartington.

Soil Association, headquartered in Bristol.

New Economics Foundation, independent 'think and do tank'.

Intermediate Technology Development Group.

Centre for Alternative Technology in Wales.

Green Books, publishing company at Dartington.

Resurgence bi-monthly magazine of 'vision and action'.

Regular Schumacher lectures are held at Bristol with the speakers and briefing authors having included Herbert Girardet, Zac Goldsmith, R.D. Laing, Michael Meacher, George Monbiot, Jonathon Porritt and Anita Roddick. Girardet, in his book *Cities People Planet: Creating Liveable and Sustainable Cities* (Wiley Academy 2004), gives a definition: 'A 'sustainable city' enables all its citizens to meet their own needs and to enhance their well-being, without degrading the natural world or the lives of other people, now or in the future.' He concluded: 'The greatest energy of cities should flow inwards, to create masterpieces of human creativity, not outwards, to draw in ever more products from ever more distant places.'

Natural Step's compass

The second organisation which seeks to encourage an ecologically conscious generation is The Natural Step UK, a branch of The Natural Step (TNS), an international charity pioneered in Sweden in 1989 by Dr Karl-Henrik Robèrt. The UK branch was established in 1997 by Forum for the Future with its purpose 'to develop and share a common framework comprised of easily understood, scientifically-based principles that can serve as a compass to guide society toward a just and sustainable future.'

Dr Robèrt, a cancer research scientist, was met in 1991 by John, who introduced him to Schumacher lectures that year. Dr Robèrt had formed a science-based framework of principles. The framework has four 'system conditions' developed in collaboration with scientists, business people, educators, politicians and communities. These conditions for a sustainable society are:

1. Fossil fuels, metals and other materials are not extracted at a faster pace than their

slow deposit into the Earth's crust.

2. Substances are not produced at a faster pace than that at which they can be broken down in nature or redeposited into the Earth's crust.

3. The productive surfaces of nature are not diminished in quality or quantity, and we must not harvest more from nature than can be created.

4. Basic human needs must be met with the most resource-efficient methods possible, including a just resource distribution.

The Natural Step UK, of which John has been a board member, is chaired by the environmentalist Jonathon Porritt, who was one of the three founders of Forum for the Future, which had been set up in 1996 to promote a sustainable way of life. JT Group is a member of the Forum Business Network.

Sustainable development, Porritt stated, 'is one of those ideas that everybody supports, but no-one really knows what it means in practice. The Natural Step process slices through that confusion, providing companies with a scientifically rigorous set of rules, using training and development techniques specifically fashioned for the business environment.'

Porritt was appointed chair of the Sustainable Development Commission, the government's independent advisory body. In its report, *Shows Promise: But Must Try Harder* (April 2004), it claimed that the government's central objective continued to be conventional economic growth, rather than the well-being of society and the planet as a whole. 'We see a world in which many natural resources are being dangerously depleted, in which biodiversity is being lost at an alarming rate, in which many forms of pollution are spreading, which is gravely threatened by long-term climate change, and in which the total impact of the UK's activity is adding to the world's problems.'

Forum for the Future itself has said: 'Our relative wealth [in the UK] may cushion us from some of the worst consequences of our own excesses, but we are already experiencing significant problems. Rural communities have been brought to their knees by an agricultural system that is almost criminally unsustainable. Our cities are clogged by the growth in traffic – something that conventional approaches by successive governments seem incapable of tackling…At the heart of these problems is our failure to realise that the environment underpins all human activity, and that we cannot sustain progress if we do so at its expense.

'Fortunately,' it added, 'a growing number of organisations and individuals are making the connection and bringing forward new ways of tackling our economic, social and environmental problems in a joined-up way. At Forum for the Future, we believe that this joined-up approach – sustainable development – is the only way to achieve the better quality of life.'

The construction industry, according to TNS, produces half of the UK's physical waste and the operation of buildings accounts for 50 per cent of total energy consumption. TNS commented on its Stepping Stones website that 'sustainable development in construction has been receiving considerable attention since publication of the Egan Report Rethinking Construction in 1998. There are a few prime examples of real 'bricks and mortar' progress to back up all the rhetoric and fine thinking. Two of the construction projects in the UK with which TNS has been involved are award winners: the new Great Western Hospital in Swindon and Wessex Water's operational HQ in Bath.' Great Western Hospital, which opened in December 2002, was built in a Private Finance Initiative project by Carillion. The company claimed it set a benchmark at the hospital for sustainable construction, consuming less energy than typical hospitals and emitting less carbon dioxide. The hospital featured in a Construction Best Practice case study sponsored by the Department of Trade & Industry.

Urban renewal

JT Group has taken a new direction in the twenty first century. Leigh Court, the mansion near Bristol which JT had owned and substantially restored, was sold in October 2004. 'This sale marks the end of an era for the group,' John Pontin reported. 'We acquired the property in 1992 and were subsequently able to create sustainable new uses for the building which should ensure its future value to the community. The major works that we carried out to the roof should also ensure that the building is sound for many years to come. We wish the new owner well!"

Its new owner was Bristol Chamber of Commerce & Initiative – the mansion had been its leased home – and formed as Business West in a merger with Bath and South Gloucestershire Chambers of Commerce and Business Link. The Initiative was evolved as the West of England Initiative to be a 'think tank' to consider and influence issues within the sub-region. Over 2,500 companies are now members of Business West which, it stated, 'is determined to unite the business community and tackle the strategic issues.'

The same year, JT created the not-for-profit company called Under the Sky. Its name evokes its broad intentions: to restore or make buildings for community purposes and to encourage public open spaces and public transport systems. The focus, it stated, 'is for local action towards a liveable and sustainable region.' Bristol, where Under the Sky has initial aims, has always been a city of contrast with its two universities, its economic strength and high-value properties – and also some of the most deprived wards in England. The historic handsome houses, especially in Clifton, and the new Harbourside developments have drawn in new residents but much of the city's suburbs remain tatty with nondescript properties. Bristol Civic Society stated: 'Rapid growth of the city's population; the enormous increase in the volume of vehicular traffic; and the technical complications of modern urban development will present the society with many problems in the future, in addition to their concern to encourage improved standards of architectural design throughout the city, and to prevent the destruction of treasures of the past by neglect, indifference, or careless planning.'

Under the Sky intends to counter conventional development – rather as conventional construction had been countered by JT since the 1960s. The new company was inspired by John Pontin, who said: 'Its principle objective is to provide development expertise and assist with the transformation of neglected buildings and sites for the benefit of the community as a whole, but which are outside the normal scope of private developers, housing associations or other organisations.'

The company, while willing to act alone, is more likely to be a development partner with community organisations, intending to proceed for community-valued purposes. 'We have chosen to be a not-for-profit company limited by guarantee in order to avoid any conflict between the needs of the project and the need to distribute profits to shareholders,' it stated. 'This also helps us to qualify as recipients for public money, lottery grants and charitable funds. Directorships of the company are unpaid.'

Under the Sky is chaired by John with fellow directors:

Richard Silverman, executive director and a visiting professor at the University of the West of England and Cardiff University specialising in urban design and regeneration. A former head of the Welsh School of Architecture, he chaired the design panel of Cardiff Bay Development Corporation, the 13-year project completed in 2000. Cardiff Bay, with its regeneration of the derelict and contaminated industrial waterfront, is an exception to urban developments which restrict public access. The corporation, acting as an intermediary, took revenue from developers to devise an agenda for open spaces, notably the Oval Basin where events are held.

Ian Cawley, a chartered surveyor with considerable experience in a wide range of development and construction projects in the UK and abroad. Since moving to Bristol in 1973 he has been involved in some of the largest developments in the region including the Mall at Cribbs Causeway and the Harbourside development in Bristol docks.

Herbert Girardet, the chairman of Schumacher UK and whose career includes being a visiting professor at the University of the West of England and director of research of the World Future Council Initiative.

David Johnstone, a chartered accountant, who has been a director of JT Group since 1979.

'The directors of the company are local people sharing ideals and bringing specific relevant skills,' Under the Sky's website stated. 'We have a history of involvement in development projects involving mixed-uses, collaborative working, charitable purposes and sustainability.' It said: 'Our motivating aim is to create futures for land and buildings that are socially responsible, environmentally sustainable and thoughtfully designed. Towards this aspiration, our objectives are to fulfil the potential of neglected but important sites where conventional development has not been able to do this; provide fitting accommodation for community organisations that would not otherwise have it; and undertake projects where significant advances can be made towards sustainable urban living.'

Shared ideals

Although JT had previously achieved cultural public places, notably Arnolfini and Waterside Media Centre, Under the Sky was 'a new concept which could be equipped to respond beyond what JT could do or had done,' Richard Silverman, its executive director, explained. 'We're interested not just in environmental and economic sustainability but in social sustainability – liveability is one of our aims. It is nothing less than a possible whole new sector in the development world.'

The new company is in a semi-detached relationship with JT which is willing to provide financial support, as well as managerial expertise, during its early stages. 'JT will still have a parenting role because it has launched it and supports it,' John said. 'But Under the Sky is different. My energies go into making it work with it focused on delivering best practice and interesting case studies around the built environment, helping to raise awareness in the general public. We're looking at the very opposite of the development process of how to maximise values. Instead, our interest is to maximise the value of the site in the community – what would the uses be, and how we could hold onto the value of existing buildings. It's a new initiative to embrace everything we do.'

Under the Sky said it would do 'the many essential and specialised things that have to be done if any piece of land is to find a new future whether as buildings, open space or for public transport use. We can buy the site from its existing owner; take the project, acting for and with the new users, through the processes that lead to a planning consent; help find the funding from public and private sources to finance the project; and employ and manage the expertise necessary to design and carry out the work.' It aimed to 'draw on the best intellectual, technical and cultural resources of the region.' It is a member of Voscur, a voluntary network in Bristol of community organisations and enterprises seeking to regenerate the city.

'Our job is to put together a scenario which reflects what local people want, gives a return to the land owner and provides uses which are congenial to the community,' Richard Silverman stated. 'We have no agenda – apart from our stated ideals – that might otherwise say 'Sorry, you've got to have houses we can sell or shops that we can let because otherwise we won't make a profit.' We're simply not in that business. What is important to us is, I hope, that people will say that Under the Sky enables them to give direct expression to their community needs.'

Big developers, Richard said, 'sometimes have an arm that does something different. Maybe they build some sustainable housing for example. There's no reason why a developer shouldn't do this and bring all their expertise but, of course, that part of their work requires a different mindset. What we would like to see in 20 years' time is that every city has organisations like Under the Sky – socially orientated developers – but they are likely only to be viable if they are each backed by a major conventional developer. We would hope for a future where local authorities and community groups are able to go to a trusted social-economy development sector that has real expertise and money behind it, but nevertheless does not have a profit agenda.

'People do sometimes say to us, 'Where's the catch?' They can't understand why we as individuals are doing this. It is here that the seniority of the directors comes in because we do not depend upon Under the Sky for our livelihood. Of course, we have to reassure people we are serious, but our track records as individuals and the availability of JT's expertise confirm this.'

JT's acquisition in 2005 of the Chew Magna mill, which is to be transformed as part of the 'zero waste' project, is in keeping with Under the Sky's intentions. In Bristol, two big sites – 'famous eyesores,' said Richard – are being actively pursued to become community-based locations. 'We cannot take speculative risks – anything we do has to have an end user before we start. Therefore, rather than seeking development opportunities, we encourage existing groups to come to us in the hope that Under the Sky can help make their ambitions possible.' One early intention has been to restore a derelict sailors' chapel for arts and community uses and another is to renovate a derelict building that could be an arts centre or covered market. There are also possibilities for developing Redcliffe Wharf – the site where the replica of Cabot's fifteenth-century ship *Matthew* was built. Discussions have been held with the Redcliffe Futures Group, a grouping of more than 20 organisations and individuals within Bristol, to help them to realise their vision of a sustainable future for the Redcliffe district. Another possibility is working with co-housing groups to bring forward the way to provide housing that matches the social and ecological ambitions of would-be owners.

Directors of Under the Sky are well aware that their initiatives are experimental. Its not-for-profit basis and collaborative working with other organisations challenge conventional ways. Development risk – usually balanced against an expected profit – has to be managed and shared. Whether this new way of working will succeed has yet to be known.

A city vision

JT Group, by 2006, had a small staff averaging just 11 people and had welcomed a new non-executive director, Peter Rilett, who had previously been senior partner at KPMG's Bristol office. The business is now run on the basis of its total return to shareholders including increases in asset values, and its profits, in the year to June 2006, were £55,000; however, equity shareholders' funds rose by £2.7m to £12m, and income-producing properties let at Bristol Harbourside were valued at £24.5m. The company, though, never just treads water at its Harbourside home of 70 Prince Street. Its motto is 'With a view to the future.'

One future is to help meet the central government's demands for most regions to create more residential accommodation wherever possible. The vision for the West of England process, which is now in a drafting stage for new housing stock, has many potential sites scattered across the sub-region of the greater Bristol conurbation which covers the former Avon county. One important opportunity is for South-west Bristol and an area of some 2,000 acres within North Somerset.

'In the past, a major problem in the greater Bristol sub-region had been the almost complete failure of strategic planning,' John Pontin said. 'The Tories broke up old Avon to replace it with the four unitary councils. But the councils would seldom want to talk together.' Recently, it has been broadly agreed by the authorities that, with Bristol as the economic engine of the West of England, the sub-region needs many new houses for its increasing population. The unitary councils have begun to co-operate in deciding where the developments should be and of what quality.

JT has a half interest in 42 acres at Ashton Vale, next to the David Lloyd sports centre and the park and ride site – which had been previously built by JT Design Build – and adjacent to a 500-acre site owned by Ashton Park Ltd. That land, which had been used before for tipping, is currently being talked about as being part of an extension to Bristol's urban fringe.

'We have our 42 acres right at the point of an arrowhead, widening towards Bristol International Airport,' John said. 'It's interesting because it's so close to the city centre and you could almost walk there from our site, in 15 minutes.'

'South-west and South Bristol should have good infrastructure, the highest sustainable development principles and the highest ideals around design,' John stated, emphasising his continuing ambitions. 'Let's have best world-class thinking around what is intelligent planning – trying to get homes, jobs, work and leisure all in the one place as much as possible – and assets and infrastructure. We want to play our part in achieving a sustainable and exciting future and to have the vision for Bristol and the West of England.'

Another and immediate future is the creation of a new restaurant and brasserie in V Shed on Bristol Harbourside. This was developed in partnership with Barny Haughton of the Quartier Vert restaurant and cookery school, and opened in the summer of 2006. It is called Bordeaux Quay and will be a showcase for the zero waste, sustainable and organic initiatives that are core to JT's philosophy.

Conclusion: public value of a private company

JT Group has always been an unconventional company, ever since it began in 1961. Like any other firm, it has a history of ups and downs, successes and failures, and profits and losses. It has proven, however, to be an innovative business, headed for more than 40 years by John Pontin, himself an original character and a philanthropic, visionary chairman.

It was one of the first British companies to revive the 'design and build' concept and its long-term partnership with contemporary cultural organisations has never been confined to short-term financial interests. Today, its ethical attitudes – fervently supported by John – have brought forward an imaginative concept of mixed-use sustainable developments to benefit local communities.

During the past decade, since the pioneering time of JT Design Build, the construction industry has changed in some respects with initiatives to encourage 'best practice'. In 1994, the Latham Report 'Constructing the Team' challenged the traditional industry's deep-rooted adversarial nature. Sir Michael Latham said: 'The industry is still a long way from adopting the most high-tech methods of communication, resulting in delay, confusion and subsequent waste.' His report led to the establishment of the Construction Industry Board to oversee reform. Subsequent initiatives were to include a response to the Egan report Rethinking Construction (1998), the organisation Constructing Excellence funded by the Department of Trade & Industry, and RIBA's Constructive Change committee.

Government and the public sector require building projects to be delivered by the Private Finance Initiative, prime contracting with supply-chain integration, and design and build which had become a mainstream procurement choice. Overall, design and build is selected for about a third of new construction. Its concept, though, has become much looser than when JT practised it. Contractors are more likely to commission architects for particular projects rather than to have in-house designers. An ever-greater proportion of building work is carried out by subcontractors. Many developers and builders continue to regard profit to be of much more importance than good design and quality.

With the population still rising in the UK, the country requires ever more buildings. Families have become smaller and more divided, with people in search of work moving away from their childhood districts. Businesses and the public sector want new premises and new locations. Villages, towns and cities need to be renovated and rebuilt but not, one hopes, in the incoherent manner of the previous century. Architects have become more conscious of producing sustainable design and with a closer involvement of local communities. However, as in the past and still today, architects are mostly selected for important buildings, company headquarters and individual properties while, all too often, they are ignored for the design of houses. Far too many homes in Britain are standard boxes with no relation to vernacular architecture.

Construction will always be a huge and cyclical sector of the economy. By 2003, total employment of the industry was over 1.1 million people and there were about 170,000 firms - although about 40 per cent of these firms were run by a single person. The industry is still male-dominated: more women have joined the architectural profession but very few women are employed in practical construction work. Training is ever more essential and there are now several universities with schools of the built environment. The University of the West of England – in the city of Bristol where JT Group is based – created a faculty of the built environment in 1992 to promote and strengthen, it said, 'the university's profile in the disciplines of architecture, planning, housing, surveying, construction, local government, urban studies, geography and environmental management.'

For the benefit of all, buildings should be designed well by architects, built well by construction companies and lived in well by their occupants, made to be comfortable with environmental advantages such as better insulation and power savings. For the sustainability of the built environment, there needs to be reduction of waste, recycling of materials, control of emissions and use of renewable energy. The temptation is to call on government to implement policies that are mandatory rather than voluntary, given that companies may be willing to accept corporate social responsibility but are often constrained by erratic share prices and earnings. Yet those who want creditable and sustainable developments should find it worthwhile to consider case histories of what has been built. In this case, there is JT Group – a private company which, in its pioneering history and its intended future, can be recognised to be of public value.

Definitions

Bill of quantities A document which itemises the materials and the required labour.

Brief A written statement of the client's requirements.

Building Regulations and statutory consents Building Regulations relate to health and safety, energy conservation and facilities for disabled people. Statutory consents may be for development control reasons, such as town and country planning, health and safety, and fire precaution.

Construction management A form of procurement in which the client enters into a contract with a construction manager, who is paid a fee for managing the work of trade contractors.

Design and build An integrated project team responsible for both design and construction. The team is expected to deliver performance benefits to the client.

Fast-tracking Fast-tracking is intended to reduce project time by the overlapping of design and construction.

Fixed-price contract A lump-sum contract based on fixed prices for units of specific work. The fixed prices might or might not be adjusted for inflation, depending on the terms of the contract.

JCT contract Joint Contracts Tribunal, established in 1931, produces standard forms of construction contracts.

Novation The client employs consultants to design and specify the project and a contractor is then selected by competition. The client novates (or transfers) his agreement with the consultants to the contractor.

Prime cost contract The contractor carries out the work for the payment of a prime cost (defined) and a fixed fee calculated in relation to the estimated amount of the prime cost.

Procurement Building procurement is the organisational structure adopted by a client for the management of the design and construction of a project.

Turnkey contract The client has an agreement with a single organisation, who provides the design and construction under one contract, and which frequently also involves land acquisition, financing and leasing.

Project Procedures

Outline proposals The client's brief is prepared with a project budget. The proposals are amended with the preparation of basic site plans and construction principles.

Draft design and construction brief The timing, complexity and procurement of the project are assessed. Some projects may have 'sub-briefs' to cover specific aspects. Most briefs will develop in stages with more detail added.

Planning consents The design forms the basis of an application for outline planning permission or the agreement of a planning brief with the local authority. Negotiations will be held with statutory authorities such as the building control inspector or the Highways Authority.

Design team The team will be dependent on the nature of the development and the skills required. The outline proposal is developed to include, for example, materials. The cost plan is updated and design revised to meet the budget and client's brief.

Detailed brief and consents Depending on the procurement route, a detailed brief may be issued. Revisions will be as required and applications made for detailed planning and building regulation consents and, if necessary, highways consent.

Detailed design The design is advanced to a level of detail ready for construction. It is revised as necessary to meet the budget and requirements of statutory authorities. The cost plan is updated.

Main contractor The main contractor will be appointed by tender. The timing will vary depending on the procurement route. Novation may take place at this stage, for example in some design and build schemes where the design team is novated from the client to the contractor.

Sub-contractors With traditional construction, sub-contractors may have agreed fixed-price contracts with the main contractor based on a detailed design prior to the start of the main contract. With construction management, trade contracts will only be tendered when necessary.

Construction and handover The project is completed and delivered to the client. Some contracts define a 'snagging' period (commonly 12 months) during which the contractor is expected to rectify any defects.

Reports

The placing and management of contracts (Simon Report 1944)

Ministry of Works party report on building (Philips Report 1950)

Survey of the problems before the construction industry (Emmerson Report 1962)

The placing and management of contracts for building and civil engineering work (Banwell Report 1964)

Communications in the building industry (Tavistock Institute 1965)

Interdependence and Uncertainty (Tavistock Institute 1966)

Large industrial sites report (NEDC 1970)

The public client and the construction industries (Wood Report 1975)

Faster building for industry (NEDO Report 1983)

Faster Building for Commerce (NEDO Report 1988)

Constructing the team (Latham Report 1994)

Technology foresight – progress through partnership (OST Report 1995)

Rethinking Construction (Egan Report 1998)

Design Review (Commission for Architecture and the Built Environment 2002)

Index